NEARING RETIREMENT

To Mum, Dad and Nan who
successfully negotiated
late working life and
found happy retirements.

Nearing Retirement

A Study of Late Working Lives

PHIL LYON
Lecturer in Sociology,
Robert Gordon's Institute of Technology

Avebury

Aldershot · Brookfield USA · Hong Kong · Singapore · Sydney

Published by

Avebury

Gower Publishing Company Limited,
Gower House, Croft Road, Aldershot, Hants GU11 3HR
England

Gower Publishing Company,
Old Post Road, Brookfield, Vermont 05036, USA

British Library Cataloguing in Publication Data

Lyon, Phil
   Nearing retirement : a study of late working
   lives.
   1. Retirement---Great Britain
I. Title
306'.38   HQ1064.G7

ISBN   0-566-05233-4

Printed in Great Britain by
Blackmore Press, Shaftesbury, Dorset

Contents

Tables

Figures

Acknowledgements

Undertaking the research on which this book is based, and writing up the material, has only been possible with support and advice from many sources.

I owe an intellectual debt to Chris Harris, my Ph.D. supervisor, whose guidance was always tactful and encouraging. Carol and Nicky Lyon gave me reasons for starting and finishing the enterprise; and conversations with Rob Bayliss, Julian Bell and Joe Hogan, colleagues at RGIT, helped to keep me going when the end seemed so far away. Julian Bell did me the great service of reading and criticising first drafts, and Anne Greig undertook the onerous task of organising and typing the final version. Needless to say, the book's imperfections are all my own work!

Finally, employees and ex-employees of Stoneywood Mill and Aberdeen District Council were more than generous with their time, information and encouragement. Their story is, I believe, an important one, and it is to be hoped that I have done justice to it.

Introduction

A PERIOD OF UNCERTAINTY

Late working life is an increasingly interesting
part of the life path. One should, perhaps, add the
qualification that it is interesting from a research
point of view because many older workers could
justly question whether uncertainty is best
described in this way.

   Older workers are on the threshold of one of the
major turning points in their lives - retirement -
the significance of which is grounded in the
pervasive influence that employment has had in the
preceding years. Like it or not, when people get
within sight of retirement the circumstances of
their work and employment have been shaping them for
a long period of time. Other than the wage packet
or salary cheque, the influences might not appear
very obvious but retirement will spotlight them.
Employment applies a timetable to the days and
weeks; provides a set of social contacts and
involves workers in activity and concerns beyond
the home (1). We might speculate, then, that in as
much as older workers consider life in retirement
some uncertainty will circumscribe the prospect.
The near future will bring changed social and

material conditions. What they will be like, in
reality, is inherently uncertain.

   Time is a potential paradox in retirement. One of
retirement's attractive features, the promise of
being able to please oneself about time, can simultaneously be one of the major problems in the sense
that something other than work has to fill that
time. What was formerly associated only with
leisure, and slipped in between the hours of work,
is set to become the framework of everyday life.
Given the experience of weekends that were never
long enough, and holidays that seemed too short, it
is hard to believe that more 'free' time could
actually create difficulties. On the other hand, if
work and passive recuperation from work have laid
claim to time during working life, then coping with
more time in a more active fashion is an untested
skill.

   Equally, retirement is likely to curtail a number
of social contacts. If an adequate circle of
friends and acquaintances exists independently of
that furnished by employment then this is, perhaps,
of relatively small importance. However, in as much
as employment has been a source of significant
social contacts who have shared the intricacies of
working life, a gap is going to be left.

   Invariably, retirement means a reduction in
income even if there is to be an occupational (2)
pension supplementing that provided by the state.
Moreover, a large proportion of older workers do not
have the prospect of an occupational pension to
cushion the fall from wage to state pension, such
provision being far from universal (3). Even when
workers enter retirement from employment that
operated a scheme, the pension may be small.
Problems associated with the transfer of pension
rights from one employer to another, or a late
start in a scheme, produce minimal benefits.

   Life in retirement is a future state clouded by
uncertainties of this kind even if the idea of
relinquishing work is an attractive one. However,
it would appear that the biggest uncertainty of late
working life is the question of how long it will
last. Over and above the possibility of health
impairment that could result in retirement earlier
than had been expected, losing employment through

redundancy or employer-initiated early retirement
is, for many, a distinct probability.

   In the late 1970s, and through the 1980s, British
employers and their employees have increasingly had
to contend with the problems of labour force
reductions. Sometimes, as with the restructuring
of British Steel, the contractions are massive,
devastating to local communities and the focus of
bitter national debate. The issue of job loss was
at the heart of the protracted strike by the
National Union of Mineworkers although the fact was
often overshadowed. Beyond such well-publicised
examples, there are many more instances of job loss
acknowledged only in provincial media output and the
changing profile of local unemployment statistics.

   Even when labour force reductions are well-
publicised, the specific role played by older workers tends to be obscured. Yet they are likely to
be over-represented among the redundancies owing to
higher entitlements and, perhaps, the greater
'social acceptability' of this arrangement in
partial redundancy programmes (4). If it is technological change that causes the redundancies then
older workers, being more closely identified with
the 'passing order' of workplace skills, are the
most likely targets. Once unemployed, older men
and women are likely to remain so for a longer time
than those ten or twenty years younger (5). Skill
redundancy and ageism are as much adversaries in the
search for work as they are in the holding of jobs.

   Furthermore, labour force reductions can be
achieved using early retirement without replacement.
Although it is virtually impossible to distinguish,
at a national level, between early retirements of
this kind and those using replacement to restructure
work forces, it is clear that in either case it is
the older worker who is vulnerable. In fact, one
could argue that there has been something of a
'quiet revolution' in employer practices regarding
older workers and the convention of working up to
the state pensionable age. One way of ascertaining
the scale of the trend towards earlier retirement is
to look at economic activity rates among, for
example, men in the 60-64 year band. General
Household Survey (6) data reveals that the rate
slipped from 85 per cent in 1973 to 63 per cent in
1983. Even in the 55-59 year category over the same

period, economic activity declined from 94 per cent to 85 per cent. It is largely these falling rates of economic activity that give the measure of trends in retirement under the state pensionable age. These changes might not excite much popular attention, but they are by no means insignificant.

The older worker is, therefore, fairly described as vulnerable in the prevailing economic circumstances. Not only are there the vagaries of ageing and ill-health to contend with, but the technological and organisational changes that invalidate experience. The net result is an increased tendency for their exclusion from the labour force via redundancy, or from the labour market in the form of early retirement. As economic activity rates include workers and the registered unemployed, the scale of change is most clearly revealed in the falling rates for those actually in work. For example, 80 per cent of the 60 - 64 year old males were working in 1973, but this had fallen to 52 per cent by 1983 (7).

Obviously, not every older worker is in precisely the same situation. Some will be less affected than others by technological and organisational change. Some jobs will not involve heavy or awkward tasks that underline the process of ageing. Even health impairment operates differentially. The extent to which a particular condition, short of major functional incapacity, jeopardises employment depends on the nature of the job, and employer capacity and willingness to redeploy older workers to more suitable work.

In short, there are going to be different kinds, and levels, of vulnerability. To explore this question of differential vulnerability, and the relationship between work experiences and feelings about retirement; this book focusses on late working life in two very different types of organisation - a paper mill and a local authority direct works department.

ABOUT THIS STUDY

Although the focus of this study is late working life, it emerged from concern with the problems of retirement. Problems and, indeed, the general circumstances of life in retirement were, it seemed, best understood in terms of the working life that had gone before. This was not altogether an original conclusion for as far back as 1954, Friedmann and Havighurst (1977) had observed that the meaning of retirement and the meaning of work were interconnected.

Work is, however, a word of many facets. It can refer to occupation, employment, or simply to activity. With Friedmann and Havighurst our attention is drawn to the occupational dimension. While valuable insights on retirement are to be gained from this perspective, it does have the effect of de-emphasising the role of employment. One might argue that life in retirement is influenced not only by the frame of meaning generated by former occupation, but by the circumstances of former employment. Among other things, control over the timing of retirement, the existence and adequacy of 'occupational' pensions and pre-retirement education are variables primarily linked to employment rather than occupation. In these matters, being a welder, for example, is less important than where the welder was employed.

With these thoughts in mind, it seemed that some exploration of later life employment might usefully contribute to our understanding of the conditions under which people embark on retirement. There had been studies by the Nuffield Foundation and the Medical Research Council in the 1950s and 1960s centred on the employment implications of human ageing; but labour market conditions were somewhat different then, and early retirement arrangements generally had undergone considerable development. Furthermore, these studies had not directly address-ed the retirement implications of what happened in the later years of employment.

It might have been possible to limit the research to one organisation and collect late working life data within a specific framework of technology, manpower policy and organisational structure. A single research setting of this kind would have raised the traditional problems of the 'case study' (8), although as Beynon and Blackburn (1972) have argued, and demonstrated, there can be advantages in this strategy. Many variables are held constant. For the present study, though, it

appeared that more advantage would be gained in a
research design that allowed contrast between employment settings.

At this juncture it would have been logical to
establish comparative criteria, and approach organisations that differed significantly in their structures and policies. Various forms of technological,
structural and policy contrast were considered, but
the fact that late working life experiences in the
two organisations featured in this study are so
different is, in part, the result of good fortune.

Among other things, problems of access (9) intervene between design and implementation and, unless
research is commissioned, sponsored or tolerated by
organisations, getting in touch with people to
interview can be a major difficulty. It was
essential that the organisations to be approached
each had a large and established workforce to allow
the possibility of reasonably sized samples; and it
was fortunate that two meeting these criteria, and
having clear technological, structural and policy
differences, were willing to assist. The interviewing arrangements put to them were, perhaps, salient
in the reception of the research proposal. The idea
was not for organisationally-based research as such,
which might have intruded on the normal routines of
work, but for access to the names and addresses of
older workers and retirees so that direct approaches
could be made for interviews in their own homes.
Both organisations were generous with this kind of
assistance.

Each was able to provide an adequate population of
current and retired male manual workers from which
samples could be generated. The late working lives
of other groups would have made for interesting
comparison, but male manual workers were of
particular interest because their vulnerability in
terms of poor health and physical arduous work had
been studied in the context of the 1950s and early
1960s but social, economic and technological changes
since that period suggested it would be worth re-
examining these late working lives.

The purpose of samples that spanned the point of
retirement was to allow a potentially better
exploration of the transition from worker to retiree
status. While those who had retired could report on

experiences in the later years of employment and, retrospectively, their feelings about retirement; it was thought that older workers would provide a triangulation on accounts of late working life, and give clearer insights into feelings about retirement from the 'other' side. Information on the experiences at Stoneywood Mill were gathered from interviews with 17 older workers and 41 retirees, of whom 21 had retired before the state pensionable age. Similarly, at Aberdeen District Council Building and Works Department, there were interviews with 16 older workers and 36 retirees, of whom 24 had taken early retirement. In all, the study involved 110 interviews.

The age limits set on the samples were somewhat arbitrary, but not entirely so as the literature had established some conventions about the onset of what has here been termed late working life. Although Pearson's (1957) study of patterns of light work acquisition had indicated the mid-forties as a starting point, Wedderburn's (1965) comments on the mid-fifties (10) suggested this to be a better approximation for the beginning of a period when career moves were more clearly age-related. Equally, following Friedmann and Havighurst (1977), it appeared there was a good chance that retirement would be emerging as a personally relevant consideration from that age.

Initially, then, the lower age limit was set at 55 years, but was marginally reduced to 54 years because both organisations had difficulty in supplying enough names in the age categories requested to compensate for non-response. In retrospect, the lower age limit was about right because even men in their mid-fifties often regarded retirement as a distant prospect. On the other hand, in the case of council workers and retirees, it was clear that many age-related career moves had occurred before that age. All considered, it was a reasonable compromise given the scale of the present study.

The top limit was notionally set at 70 years. Although there was some assurance in the literature (Musto and Benison, 1969; Thompson, 1971) that distortions of memory were unlikely to be a problem in relation to significant factual matters; it was not prudent to subject the study to doubts on this point by extending too far the period of recall. In the event, it was necessary to interview some retirees in their early seventies, but most were in their mid-to-late sixties. Stoneywood Mill retirees had a mean average age of 65.1 years at the time of interview, and a mean average retirement of 2.2 years. The Building and Works retirees closely matched this profile at 64.8 years and 2.9 years respectively. Arguably, then, such men were in a good position to comment on the transition from work to retirement.

The interviews, carried out between October 1981 and October 1983, illustrated the organisational factors that promote or inhibit employment to the state pensionable age. Equally, they underline the point that the conditions of later life employment have a bearing on retirement. Although this study can only be regarded as exploratory, hopefully it does something to redress the neglect of these issues.

NOTES

(1) For further discussion of the significance of employment, see Jadoda (1982).

(2) This term is something of a misnomer as such pensions are primarily related to employment rather than occupation.

(3) See Tables 7.46, 7.47, 7.48, 7.49 and 7.50 in General Household Survey 1983 (1985).

(4) For discussion of the relationship between age and redundancy, see Caséy and Bruche (1983, pp. 55-59).

(5) Table 4.22 of Social Trends (1986) shows that, in April 1985, 60.5 per cent of male claimants aged 50 to 59 years were unemployed for more than a year. For female claimants over the age of 50 years, the figure was 58.5 per cent.

(6) These data are drawn from Table 7.2, General Household Survey 1983 (1985).

(7) These same economic activity figures (see note 6) distinguish between those working and those who are registered as unemployed.

(8) For discussion of 'case study' limitations, see Blau, P. (1973, pp. 3-6) and White and Trevor (1983), pp. 14-19, 147-150).

(9)   See Becker (1977, pp. 14-23) for an outline of neglected problems of method.

(10)   Wedderburn (1965, p. 85) makes the point that, in the aftermath of redundancy, it is the actual and supposed health circumstances of men in their mid-fifties that limits their chances of employment.

1 Age and employment vulnerability

In Britain, most of us have grown used to the idea that, short of an early death, we will retire from work. Although this expectation, especially in terms of a pensioned period of retirement, has fairly recent origins; it has become firmly entrenched. Furthermore, because they are payable at 60 years for women and 65 years for men, state pensions have fostered a convention for the 'normal' age of retirement.

Conventional wisdom about the point of retirement is, however, rapidly becoming a poor guide to reality. Recession-induced demanning and skill redundancy have made many older workers highly vulnerable prior to the state pensionable age. New mechanisms have emerged to provide an earlier departure from the labour market.

In this chapter there is an examination of these issues, and a questioning of the extent to which retirement research has drawn on late working life employment experiences for explanation of attitudes towards retirement. With some exceptions, it is argued that our understanding of retirement is singularly uninformed by such considerations.

INSTITUTIONALISATION OF THE EXIT FROM WORK

The increased pace of technological change (Landes, 1969) has resulted in a shortening of the cycle of skill utility and skill redundancy. The role of the ageing worker in the labour force has, consequently, been modified considerably. As Ward, R. (1979) indicates, rapid technological change and the increased proportion of white-collar occupations have created an hiatus in the traditional relationship between skill accomplishment and skill transmission. For the employer, the ageing worker's long-term skill consolidation is an attribute of declining worth in the face of cumulative process modifications and shifts in the balance of work activities.

This contrasts with the situation in less technologically advanced societies:

> For an older working man of the nineteenth century and even well beyond, all that happened would have been that his periods of unemployment grew more protracted until at last he stopped looking for a job altogether. (Clark,F., 1966, p. 22)

While it can be argued that technological development per se reduces the prospects for older workers, the argument has to be qualified. Even in pre-industrial societies the continuity of useful productive activity was not always experienced. Moore (1978), for example, argues that the modern African clerical worker, on his retirement, and his grandfather moving out of a warrior age-grade, have more in common in terms of occupational discontinuity than either does with the ageing Chagga farmer who could maintain productive activity in some form until death or incapacity intervened.

The suggestion is, rather, that certain types of occupation common in pre-industrial societies but existing only to a limited extent in industrial society provide opportunity for a smooth transition into old age. In this vein, rural occupations are the strongest link between the two societal forms. Miller (1963) attributes agriculture with a range of structured opportunities.

The agricultural industry is unlike
many others since it can offer a
variety of skilled and semi-skilled
occupations differing widely in
tempo, physical demand and responsibility, and a thoughtful and
appreciative farmer is usually able
to find his older worker full-time
occupation that will not be an undue
tax on his physical and mental powers.
(Miller, 1963, p. 59)

Additionally, occupationally-related enterprises
such as gardening and small-holding, plus opportunities for part-time work meant that, in Miller's
sample, 72 per cent of 'retired' men were engaged
in a pattern of work continuity that extended to
the final incapacities of old age. A similar
perspective on continuity in a rural setting is
reported by Twente (1970):

... limited changes have taken place
in the traditional attitudes of small-
community older persons towards work.
They tend to continue to feel that work
should be terminated for reasons of
health only. Thus, whenever opportunities are available, as in the case
of a self-employed farmer, work, full-
time or part-time, continues as long
as enough physical strength can be
mustered.
(Twente, 1970, p. 38)

Industrial society's developing spectrum of
occupations present fewer opportunities for the
continuity of economic activity to a point where
incapacity limits involvement. In fact, we might
regard the existence of a period between the incapacity of old age and the end of regular economic
activity as one of the hallmarks of an advanced
industrial society. However, the early experiences
of this new period in the life course would have
been anything but pleasant, contaminated as it was
by poor health and poverty.

The diminished utility of a growing number of
older workers led only slowly to a policy infrastructure which accommodated those made dependent
in their later years, in spite of the conceptualis-

ation of old age as 'enfeeblement' (Phillipson, 1977; 1982). Along with that somewhat haphazard policy development, came the idea of a fixed retirement age applying to ever-greater sections of the working population. The emergence of a fixed retirement age may, as Thane (1978) remarks;

> ... have reflected a popular belief that
> most people became old and unfit for
> regular work at some point in their
> early sixties.
> (Thane, 1978, p. 234)

However, the institution of a fixed age of retirement was less a dispensation of altruism than a pragmatic strategy for handling the problem of diminished utility in the workplace.

> Although some of the pressure for fixed-
> age and pensionable retirement came from
> an awareness that a society richer than
> ever before should improve its provision
> for the aged poor, the crucial explan-
> ation lay in the growing demands for
> greater labour efficiency and increased
> productivity. In the face of foreign
> competition towards the end of the
> nineteenth century, the labour process
> was intensifying to increase productiv-
> ity in a number of occupations such as
> mining, textiles and engineering. Trade
> unionists complained that this led to
> the earlier redundancy of men too old
> to work at the required pace. Employers
> both introduced occupational pensions
> and pressed for a state scheme to allow
> them to lay off older workers with a
> clear conscience.
> (Parker, 1982, p. 17/18)

Fixing the age of retirement did not solve the problem of older workers' diminished utility entirely but standardising the age of entry into retirement, it could be argued, simultaneously served to strengthen the older worker's position.

> If a worker is to be arbitrarily
> released from employment at the
> age of sixty-five, his chances of
> being kept in employment until he
> is sixty-five are immeasurably
> increased. Given no system of

4

retirement whatsoever and with it no
sense of obligation on the part of
employers to keep workers on to a
certain age, the effect would be ...
to reduce the number of workers in
employment who had not yet attained
the age of sixty-five.
(Clark, S.D., 1959, p. 74)

This is, however, a better reflection of the
truth for an older worker already in employment than
it is for older workers in the labour market
generally, for there is a persistent theme of long-
term unemployment among older workers even at time
of high labour demand (International Labour
Organisation, 1954). As Wedderburn (1976)
comments:

Older workers are always heavily represented among the unemployed; and although
there is no conclusive evidence to
support the view that age and ability
are related in any absolute sense, we
do know that social institutions and
structural changes in the economy combine
to place older workers particularly at risk.
Redundancies occur first in contracting
industries which tend to have an older
labour force ... In addition, many
employers are prejudiced against older
workers and even find it cheaper to
replace an older man with a younger
one.
(Wedderburn, 1976, p. 362)

Nevertheless, at times of high labour demand while
older workers might, through skill redundancy, ill-
health, or age discrimination find re-employment
difficult if not impossible, there is an increased
tendency for the fixed retirement age to be dis-
regarded. This observation is central to
Phillipson's (1977; 1982) thesis that, in industrial society, older people are used as a reserve of
labour to be retained in employment when there are
labour shortages and, conversely, encouraged to
cease employment when there is a slump through
mechanisms such as strict adherence to the fixed
retirement age, early retirement opportunities and
labour market conditions which make late working
life unemployment long-term or permanent.

The effect of high labour demand on retirement practices is evident in Toshi's (1979) cameo of the Japanese situation in the 1970s. There was a reported widespread continuation of working life encouraged by labour shortages, increased capacity and demographic factors in Japanese society. While the age of retirement was 55 years, the 1970 Japanese Population Census indicated that 92 per cent of males between 55 and 59 years, 84 per cent of those between 60 and 64 years, and 54 per cent of males aged 65 years and over were still working. In part, this was accounted for by a considerable element of self-employment in these particular age groups, but also by the process of re-employment which may have involved status and income reductions in comparison to the job held at 55 years. There are indications (Denselow, 1983) that this parad-oxical situation of a fixed retirement age that is lower than that which the labour market can sustain, is a continuing feature of Japanese society.

Britain, however, has had the mirror-image of this problem since the latter half of the 1960s. It is, furthermore, a problem that has grown since the late 1970s. The economy has failed to expand at a rate that would absorb new entrants to the labour force.

> So, even without any decline in the demand for labour, the job gap is likely to increase in the 1980s because of the growing labour supply; estimates suggest that at least 800 new jobs a day are required to hold declining demand and rising supply at present levels of balance. (Showler & Sinfield, 1981, p. 6)

In fact, industrial recession has lowered the demand for labour and, in the midst of such trends, older workers are particularly vulnerable. Economic activity rates for men between 60 and 64 years, for example, show a marked downward progression from 85 per cent in 1973 to 63 per cent in 1983 (General Household Survey (1983), 1985). This means that, currently, over a third of the men in this age group are economically inactive, i.e. they are retired or permanently sick (1). Discussion of this trend for the years 1975 to 1978 (Employment Gazette, April 1980) shows that the proportion of men inactive through illness remained fairly constant, and that growth in the economically inactive category was almost totally attributable to increases in the number of early retirals.

Early retirement, i.e. retirement before the state pensionable age, is therefore a growing phenomenon but it has not been brought about by any formal reduction in the 'official' retirement age. It has been facilitated by employers under the provisions of their occupational pension schemes and, paradoxically, by government in the state Job Release Scheme. Further, changes in the administrative arrangements for older unemployed men effectively add another route to early retirement.

Occupational early retirement schemes

McGoldrick and Cooper (1978) noted, in their discussion of early retirement, that as recently as 1976 only 12 per cent of companies with occupational pension schemes surveyed by the National Association of Pension Funds had a 'normal' retirement age of less than 60 years for women, and 65 years for men. However, early retirement was possible on ill-health grounds, and broad interpretations were likely if the employers' interests were best served by this. By 1978, the authors were able to comment on the development of wider early retirement opportunities in such pension schemes:

> Pension schemes frequently now contain a
> provision for early retirement on a
> voluntary basis, if the company gives
> consent, while other schemes go even
> further providing for early retirement
> 'by right' ... Some encourage them to
> take up their rights. Other organis-
> ations are beginning to use voluntary
> early retirement 'schemes' or 'exercises',
> encouraging early retirement as staffing
> reductions demand or on a regular basis.
> (McGoldrick and Cooper, 1978, p. 26)

Indeed, by 1978, the data collected by the National Association of Pension Funds showed a marked change:

> Most occupational pension schemes (95 per
> cent according to a survey in 1978 by the
> National Association of Pension funds) also
> provide for employees to retire early other
> than on account of ill-health.
> (Employment Gazette, April 1980, p. 369)

Such schemes blurred the distinction between
redundancy and early retirement as use of the latter
for labour force reductions gave certain advantages
to employers (Ward, S., 1981), in terms of speed,
ease and general acceptability.

> In either its voluntary or compulsory
> form, it has been found to be a more
> acceptable alternative to redundancy,
> specifically among younger men, having
> a significantly less detrimental
> effect on workforce morale and not
> considered to bear the same stigma or
> cause the problems associated with
> redundancy.
> (McGoldrick and Cooper, 1978, p. 26)

Occupational pension schemes, where they are in
operation, have been quite openly used, therefore,
as mechanisms for removing older workers from the
labour force of a particular employer. They do
not, however, necessarily remove the older person
from the labour market because they are not paid on
the condition that no further work is undertaken,
although tax disincentives, and the limited availability of work opportunities elsewhere in the
labour market, make re-entry problematic.

The Job Release Scheme

The scheme, introduced for Assisted Areas (2) in
1977, was designed to encourage older workers to
leave the labour market. However, it was primarily
a device to reduce unemployment by making it a
condition that the state would finance this
'premature' retirement only if the firm simultaneously engaged someone who was registered as
unemployed. The intended effect was to remove an
older worker from the 'economically active' category
and provide employment for a younger person who was
'economically active' but unemployed. Thus, a two-
fold benefit to the manpower statistics was
envisaged.

From an employer's point of view, the scheme is
only of value if the organisation has need for
'replacement' workers (Department of Employment,
1981; 1984). It is useful only to employers
seeking to restructure their workforce in terms of
age and/or skill, not to those seeking labour force
reductions.

The Job Release Scheme has been effective with the most vulnerable of older workers, the unskilled and semi-skilled in areas of high unemployment (Casey & Bruche, 1983, p. 122). Furthermore, a survey conducted for the Department of Employment in 1979, revealed that 30 per cent of applicants had a ... 'long-standing illness, disability or infirmity' (Employment Gazette, April 1980, p. 368).

As Casey and Bruche point out, the Job Release Scheme:

> ... must be seen as a temporary and counter-cyclical measure rather than an early retirement policy in its own right.
> (Casey and Bruche, 1983, p. 121)

It cannot be considered as an early retirement policy in any general sense because, firstly, it is clearly selective in terms of its eligibility criteria. Application is only open to full-time workers (at least 30 hours a week) who have been in work with one employer for at least a year; and participation is voluntary for both employer and employee (Department of Employment, 1981; 1984). Secondly, the eligibility criteria, mainly age thresholds, have been subject to a number of alterations, in both directions, since 1977. It has, therefore, all the appearances of a short-term regulatory device rather than a long-term early retirement mechanism.

The Job Release Scheme is more effective, in its conditions, at ensuring the removal of older workers from the labour market than are occupational pension schemes on their own (3) for, while it does not disallow the receipt of an occupational pension (4) all the allowance is withheld if earnings are more than £4 per week. Whilst the recipient is able to leave the scheme (5), the earnings rule provides a considerable disincentive for even highly margin-alised involvement in the labour market.

While occupational pension schemes, allowing early retirement on grounds other than poor health, and the Job Release Scheme are directionally congruent in their removal of older workers from the labour force of a particular employer; they do not provide identical effects for employers, or the

labour market. As shown in Table 1.1 below, the two
mechanisms have differing effects in terms of labour
force reductions; have broadly similar effects in
allowing labour force flexibility; and differing
effectiveness in securing an end to the older person's
labour market participation - at least in the
'white' economy.

Table 1.1

Comparison between employer early retirement
provision and the Job Release Scheme

	Occupational pension schemes' early retire- ment provisions	Job Release Scheme
Allows labour force reductions	YES	NO
Allows labour force flexibility	YES	YES (If replace- ment is 'indirect')
Labour market participation of older person after early retirement	Not disallowed but taxation might be a disincentive	Considerable disincentives built into the scheme

Early retirement in all but name

There is a third mechanism whereby older workers are
given financial inducements to leave the labour
force of a particular employer. The result is not,
technically, early retirement because the older
person remains economically active but is so,
effectively, because local labour market conditions
will often ensure unemployment up to the state
pensionable age.

   This situation comes about by the operation of
the Redundancy Payments Act (1965), the aim of
which was:

      ... to facilitate ... labour mobility
      by providing statutory payments to
      employees no longer needed in the older/

> declining industries so that the
> compensation for the loss of their jobs
> would make transfer into the areas of
> industrial growth more acceptable to them.
> (Department of Employment Gazette,
> September 1978, p. 1032)

The aim of the redundancy legislation was labour
redeployment but, when allied to the idea that
excluding older workers from the labour force was
preferable to redundancies among younger people, it
has meant that the Act has been applied differentially according to age, thus creating (for older
workers) a form of quasi-early retirement.

Payments to workers declared redundant were based
on the worker's age, weekly pay and length of
service. So, in theory, it was more expensive to
make older workers redundant. However, for the
first two years of the Act's operation, provisions
actually favoured the dismissal of older workers.
The higher cost of making older people redundant
was offset by age-related refunds from a Redundancy
Fund financed by employer contributions. Where
workers over the age of 41 years were declared
redundant, seven-ninths of the cost to employers was
refunded as against two-thirds of the cost of
redundancies among younger workers. Although the
level of rebate was made uniform at 50 per cent in
1969, and reduced to 41 per cent in 1977, the effect
on the age pattern of redundancies established in
the first two years of operation was minimal.

> ... [Alteration to the structure and level
> of refunds] ... in effect transferred the
> 'age' premium from the Redundancy Fund
> to the employer, and should have acted as
> a disincentive to making older/long
> service workers redundant. Evidence of
> the results of these reductions is
> imperfect, but what there is suggests
> they had no noticeable effect on the
> established pattern.
> (Department of Employment Gazette,
> September 1978, p. 1033)

The reason for age-related redundancy patterns, as
suggested by a British Institute of Management survey into company practices (British Institute of
Management, 1974), was firmly geared to the larger

amounts   of compensation older workers would
receive:

> If the blow of redundancy could fall more
> softly on the older man, his departure
> might mean it did not have to fall at all
> on a younger, more productive, recent
> recruit. As a result, for many older
> workers the mobility the Redundancy
> Payments Act facilitated was mobility
> out of the active labour force.
> (Department of Employment Gazette,
> September 1978, p. 1033)

Late working life unemployment can, particularly
in areas of generally high unemployment, last until
the state pensionable age is attained. There is
evidence to suggest that once unemployed, older
people usually stay unemployed for a longer period
of time than those who are younger. Department of
Employment figures (Social Trends, 1986) for the UK
in April 1985 show that long term unemployment (over
52 weeks) is a problem for young and old alike. In
the case of 20 - 24 year old unemployed males, 38.9
per cent had been without work for at least a year.
However, among 55 - 59 year old unemployed males,
the figure was 60.5 per cent. In fact, 41.0 per
cent of that total relates to those out of work for
more than two years.

The de facto similarity between late working life
unemployment and early retirement is enhanced by
two further considerations. Firstly, a recent
analysis in the Employment Gazette concluded
that ... 'the longer a person is unemployed, the
less his or her liklihood of ceasing to be unemployed' (Employment Gazette, February 1984, p. 65).
Thus, late working life unemployment is not just
long, but the chances of it ending diminish with
time. Secondly, three pieces of administrative
action have further entangled the concepts of late
working life unemployment and early retirement.
In 1975, contribution conditions necessary for a
full pension at state pensionable age were eased to
allow contributions to be missed for 10 per cent
of the working life - almost five years for a man -
rather than the 4 per cent that had previously
obtained. The effect of this was to ... 'remove
the necessity for many older unemployed workers to
register for National Insurance credits once

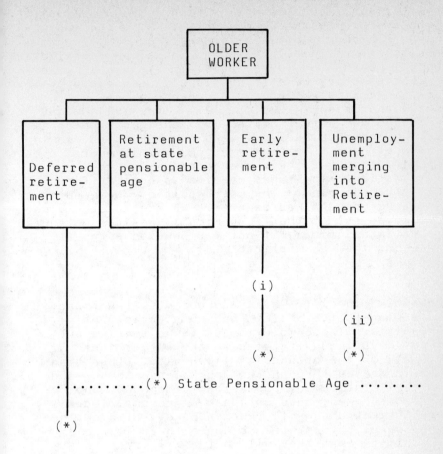

Notes:

(i)   Job Release Scheme with or without linkage to health or disability factors. Early retirement via provisions of occupational pension scheme only, may include health/disability factor.

(ii)   Unemployment merges into retirement as a result of administrative conventions after 52 weeks or, particularly in the case of women, via lapsed registration as unemployed. Pension, as such, is only payable at the state pensionable age.

Figure 1.1 Patterns of withdrawal
from the labour market

unemployed benefit was exhausted' (Employment
Gazette, April 1980, p. 367). Since November 1981,
unemployed men between the ages of 60 and 64 years
who have been out of work for more than a year have
been able ...' in return for no longer registering
themselves as unemployed, to claim the higher rate
of Supplementary Benefit previously accorded only to
the long-term sick and old age pensioners' ...
(Casey and Bruche, 1983, p. 125). The 1983 Budget
furthered the effect of the 1975 changes by clearly
stating that jobless men, aged 60 - 65 years, would
no longer have to register at an Unemployment
Benefit Office if their sole purpose was to accum-
ulate National Insurance credits to qualify for a
full state pension. The net result of these administrative changes has been to take many of the older
unemployed out of the 'economically active' category
and for statistical, if not for pension purposes,
to regard them as 'retired' (6).

Discussion

The rising levels of early labour market withdrawal
are achieved, therefore, through a variety of
mechanisms. The complexity of the situation outlined above is understated to the extent that
retirals on the grounds of ill-health, other than
those effected through the Job Release Scheme and
the early retirement provisions of occupational
pension schemes, have not been discussed. Equally,
unemployment among older women constitutes another
type of 'exit from work' because there is the
possibility that they will not register as unemployed and enter retirement via the housewife role
(7). The intention has been, however, to chart the
main innovations in early retirement rather than
exhaust all theoretical possibilities.

  The actual state retirement age has not, in all
this, been reduced. For official purposes, the
'institutionalised' exit point remains, for men
65 years, and for women 60 years. Given the mount-
ing levels of unemployment, however, the call for a
formal reduction in the state pensionable age has
not gone unheard, but even one of its most
persistent proponents (T.U.C., circa 1981) has
recognised the difficulty of financing a reduction
to a pensionable age of 60 years for all workers
when the benefit to the unemployed would be only
partial (8).

The double-bind in which policy innovation finds
itself, i.e. the desirability of a formal reduction
in the retirement age for its effect on the levels
of unemployment set against the cost of such a move,
could be solved, it is argued (Walker, 1982), by the
wider implementation of flexible retirement arrangements. Flexible retirement refers to the possibility
of entering retirement on an official state-pension-
able basis at an age other than 60 or 65 years.
Some flexibility is already built into the administrative system in terms of the newer conventions
applied to older, long-term unemployed people; and
the Job Release Scheme for older employed persons.
Additionally, flexibility in deferring retirement
is allowable; the state pension being paid at a
higher rate when retirement eventually takes place.
While discussion of flexible retirement usually
centres on increased possibilities for retirement
under the age of 65 (or 60) years; it is a concept
which spans the current state pensionable age, and
suggests a greater flexibility in the 'phasing out'
of work and the 'phasing in' of retirement for
individuals using a system of partial pensions (9).

The prognosis for this is not good in terms of an
abolition of the current state pensionable age but
maintenance, and even extension, of the present
piece-meal arrangements is likely:

> The likelihood in Britain is that the
> pressure will grow for early retire-
> ment options, rather than a statutorily
> reduced pension age ...
> (Evans, 1979, p. 34)

The exit from work looks set to remain in much its
present form for some time to come (Growing Older,
1981) although it is almost certain that early
retirement, and its de facto equivalent of late
working life unemployment are likely to increase.
In practice, therefore, the institutionalised exit
points of 65 years for men, and 60 years for women,
will be augmented rather than replaced by alternative exit routes (10).

LATE WORKING LIFE

Retirement, while it is an institutionalised
phenomenon, is the end result of several distinct
routes out of the labour market. These routes have

their origins in late working life. What happens to
older workers, in the period preceding the statutory
retirement age, depends on individual and organisational circumstances. They way that these circumstances interrelate influences not only the timing and
the mode of retirement, but also shapes the nature
of late working life.

Age and the ability to work

The relationship between age and physiological/
psychological changes is somewhat elusive. In the
first place, there is little certainty as to the
exact nature of the process of physiological ageing
(Bromley, 1974; The Economist, 10 January 1981).
Secondly, no uniform chronology can apply as
individuals vary considerably in the extent to
which the process manifests itself at specific ages.

   So, while physiological and psychological changes
can be demonstrated and related to the chronological age (Bromley, 1974) a precise taxonomy of
change and age is virtually impossible. Equally,
'ageing' is as much a social as a biological phenomenon. It is important to distinguish between
that which is inherent in human life, i.e. the
biological basis for changes, and the meanings such
changes have in a given social context. In this
respect, Ward's (1979) distinction between
intrinsic and reactive effects is useful. The
former refer to changes which are the natural
accompaniment of ageing irrespective of social
context; and the latter to individual and societal
reactions to the intrinsic effects. The interpenet-
ration of these two dimensions bedevils comment on
human ageing at any point on the life-path. Mead
(1966), who was concerned with the early part of the
life course, regarded her major problem as that of
disentanglement, while Simic (1978) criticises the
'universality' implications associated with our
approach to understanding the changes experienced
by older people.

     Even a cursory perusal of worldwide
     ethnographic literature reveals that
     aging assumes a variety of forms
     depending upon the context in which
     it occurs.
     (Simic, 1978, p. 101)

16

This is as true at the level of the employing
organisation as it is at the societal level. While
intrinsic changes take place, what they mean to the
individual worker, and his employer, depend on the
work context. Changes in muscular strength and
visual perception (Bromley, 1974) may occur without
significant effect on the employability of a person
engaged in, say, non-manual tasks, but may put the
employment of another in some jeopardy if such
abilities are central to the work task. The most
extreme examples of age-related decline affecting
employability are presented by certain types of
professional sport.

> Unlike most, a ball player must confront
> two deaths. First, between the ages of
> thirty and forty he perishes as an
> athlete. Although he looks trim and
> feels vigorous and retains unusual
> co-ordination, the superlative reflexes,
> the major league reflexes, pass on.
> At a point when many of his classmates
> are newly confident and rising in
> other fields, he finds he can no
> longer hit a very good fast ball or
> reach a grounder four strides to his
> right. At thirty-five he is
> experiencing the truth of finality.
> (Kahn, 1973, p. xviii/xix)

Even in such worlds things do not remain static:

> In the old days you used to get players
> playing till they were thirty-four or
> thirty-five. Not now. You see now,
> when they're thirty, they're virtually
> shattered. Especially in mid-field,
> running around for six or seven years.
> And they say, 'Oh, he's no good. He's
> twenty-nine now.' And they do look old
> at that age now, people in football.
> (Musgrove and Middleton, 1981, p. 50)

Similarly in more prosaic surroundings, intrinsic
changes can lead to employment problems, but their
impact is context-dependent. Brown's (1957)
laboratory study of paced task performance involving
men of various ages concluded that:

> ... a pace set for men in their twenties
> and thirties can be maintained in the

> forties but with an effort which would
> seem likely to cause strain. For people
> in their fifties this appears to be no
> longer possible.
> (Brown, 1957, p. 20)

Furthermore, Conrad's (1955) observations suggest
that the nature of the pacing is important. If
there was a degree of flexibility in the pacing of
the task, so that ... 'momentary slowness in one
cycle' could ... 'be redeemed in the next' (Brown,
1957, p. 20) then performance comparable with
unpaced work was possible. Thus, workers are less
disadvantaged by their age in work environments
that require unpaced efforts, or are paced with a
certain amount of flexibility, than are workers in
conditions where tasks are strictly paced.

Along with physiological changes associated with
chronological ageing, health circumstances may
change in later working life; and although
conceptually distinguishable, they are often inter-
related in practice. Health or combined effects
are visible in industrial survival and absenteeism
rates, although considerable caution needs to be
used with interpretation of the latter.

Industrial survival rates refer to the proportion
of workers, in a labour force, surviving from one
age category to successive ages. Clark's (1957a)
study of bus drivers and conductors employed by the
London Transport Executive is useful as an example
because the health of workers was systematically
monitored giving firmer data for industrial
survival rates than would be the case in many other
work organisations. Even here, though, the records
proved imperfect for separating health and age
effects but Clark was able to conclude that:

> ... not many of the drivers or conductors
> leave on their own initiative in their
> early sixties. But by the time they had
> reached sixty-five years rather more than
> 20 per cent of the drivers in the LTE
> statistics, as traced from the age of
> sixty, had gone through death or for
> medical and allied reasons.
> (Clark, F., 1957a, p. 12)

Even on a time-scale stopping well short of the
state pensionable age, a clear pattern of attrition

was visible with 14 per cent of the drivers and 15 per cent of the conductors employed at the age of 60 having left through ill-health, or had died, by 63 years.

Although Clark does not make a detailed age-analysis of absence he does indicate that:

> The days of absence tend among men past middle life to increase with the years ... It may, then, simply be noted that a number of ageing busmen are subject to bouts of bronchitis, fibrositis or gastritis of increasing frequency and often of increasing duration.
> (Clark, F., 1957a, p. 17)

Similarly, Wedderburn (1965) reported high levels of absence from work among older men on the grounds of health. However, the incidence of such absence for more than one month in the preceding year was higher for the 50 - 59 year olds than it was for those aged 60 years and over. This could, however, perhaps be explained in industrial survival terms, i.e. the cohort, now 60 years and over, had been depleted by death and health retirements giving them the appearance of being less subject to health-related absence whereas, in reality, they were a 'select' group of survivors.

It is not just medically-validated poor health that presents a potential problem to older workers; industrial senescence is a compounding factor. As Clark pointed out in a study of older men in the building industry (Clark, F., 1954), there are problems other than overt ill-health, and he uses the term industrial senescence to describe incongruities between the results of physiological ageing and the demands of the work situation that the older worker ordinarily has to cope with. Thus, the older worker need not be in poor health, as such, but finds it increasingly difficult to maintain job performance.

The problems of industrial senescence result, where circumstances allow, in the search for more manageable work situations. Pearson (1957) reported in her account of late working life in a Liverpool factory where the production work was predominantly unskilled or semi-skilled, and where 51 per cent of the jobs had been officially

classified as medium to heavy in their physical
demands on workers, that there were clear age-
related patterns of internal labour mobility. In
the production departments it was found that 54.8
per cent of the men had made a clear move from
heavy to lighter work, and many of the remainder,
while not changing their actual job classification,
had moved to less demanding work. A series of such
transitions took place between the ages of 45 and
65 years although the timing, and the number of
steps in the progression, varied among individuals.
There was a related movement from shift to day work
as the men aged. At 45 years, only 23 per cent
were on day work, but by the time they were 60 to
65 years, 69 per cent were deployed on day work.
Objective health problems were not the dominant
reason behind these mobility patterns, a more
subtle process was involved:

> ... transfer was often preceded by a
> period of increasing awareness of
> strain on the part of the men them-
> selves or their supervisors, even
> where there was no evidence of
> definite disability or illness ...
> (Pearson, 1957, p. 84)

Additionally, Elliott (1966), while not demonstrating anything like this pattern of age-related
movement to physically lighter work, did show that
older workers were likely to be moved to more
solitary jobs.

> ... solitary workers are significantly
> older than workers who are members of
> groups, and this may be one way in
> which pacing stress is alleviated for
> these older men.
> (Elliott, 1966, p. 235)

It was further noted by Elliott that the process
was largely informal and that supervisors played
a key role in the matching of men to appropriate
jobs.

> Since this was not mentioned by foremen
> or supervisors as a means consciously
> used to ease the burden for older men,
> it would appear to be an example of
> informal mobility, and that the older
> men tend to gravitate towards solitary
> work in the day to day allocation of

            jobs. Once on such jobs, they tend to
            remain there, to their own satisfaction
            as well as that of their younger
            colleagues, who are then enabled to
            increase their bonus earnings without
            being hampered by older men.
            (Elliott, 1966, p. 235)

A willingness to re-deploy men in this way is
partly explained by conventions relating to employment (Clark, S.D., 1959) even if this falls well
short of 'paternalism'. Furthermore, older manual
workers are not without compensatory qualities from
a managerial or supervisory point of view.

   Interviews conducted in a variety of manufacturing firms (Clark, F., 1963) revealed that the
qualities of conscientiousness and good time-
keeping more than balanced supervisors' doubts on
the older worker's productivity. While Clark
questioned the extent to which tolerance had
displaced objective assessment, his analysis of
terms used in connection with older workers showed
that negative comments occurred in only 27.7 per
cent of his discussions. Similarly, Heron and
Chown (1961) found that older, semi-skilled workers
were described as awkward, grumpy, less adaptable,
or less confident by only 17 per cent of managers
and supervisors. Responsibility, reliability,
conscientiousness, reasonableness and loyalty were
far more frequent epithets. However, some caution
is needed with the interpretation of this kind of
'personal qualities' assessment. They are,
arguably, reactive rather than intrinsic effects of
ageing. For, as some of Clark's (1963) foremen
recognised, the qualities they identified in older
workers were probably responses to fears about job
security. In short, their perceptions of vulnerability influenced their conduct.

Changing employment circumstances

Such assessments highlighted qualities most useful
to employers in stable work circumstances. In the
context of change, virtues such as steadiness and
experience are arguably less important than the
perceived vices of inflexibility and slower adjustment. The problem of industrial senescence is

invariably more complex than worker decline in
relation to the unchanging demands of an unchanging
workplace. If the ageing worker is confronted by
changes that invalidate experience, or changed
physical demands that make former coping strategies
inadequate, the solution may be found in the
internal labour mobility of later working life,
described above, but the process necessarily relies
on the availability of suitable opportunities.
Even in the 1950s, however, the shortage of
'appropriate niches' was becoming apparent. Heron
(1957) warned that the increased proportion of
older workers in industry was exhausting the traditional avenues of transfer to less demanding or
physically lighter work. In that same period, a
study based on the domestic furniture industry
(Clark, F., 1957b) noted that while repair and
conversion work was an established area for
'reliable old operatives', it accounted for little
more than 1 per cent of the total manual labour
force employed there.

   While technological change, or more specifically,
process innovation, might have no clear role in the
reduction of employment opportunities overall
(Terborgh, 1970); it undoubtedly has labour displacement effects which increases the vulnerability
of the older worker (Rothwell and Zegveld, 1979).
Experience becomes invalidated as new skills are
demanded (Mann and Williams, 1967) or, in mechanised
production processes, the emphasis of work moves
from skill to speed, and from autonomy to dominat-
ion by the process:

> For the worker, the concept of skill
> is traditionally bound up with craft
> mastery - that is to say, the combination
> of knowledge of materials and processes
> with the practiced manual dexterities
> required to carry out a specific branch
> of production ... What is left to
> workers is a reinterpreted and woefully
> inadequate concept of skill: a
> specific dexterity, a limited and
> repetitive operation, speed as
> skill ...
> (Braverman, 1974, pp. 443 - 444)

Although new technology, applied to production
processes, does not need to result in this bleak
scenario, i.e. it can lighten the work and still

demand levels of skill that workers find satisfying
(Hull et al, 1982), older workers are still vulnerable on the re-training question. At a company
level, the re-training of older workers might
produce a good result, but take longer (Smith, J.,
1974). The real question, however, is not whether
older workers can be re-trained, but will they be
re-trained. Given that process innovation in a
specific organisational setting usually means a
reduction in the required numbers of workers
necessary to maintain, or increase, production
levels, redundancies and early retirements are
common.

   The older workers' vulnerability is not, however,
limited to situations involving process innovation.
Hunter, Reid and Boddy (1970) identify 3 additional
causes of labour displacement: structural change
where an industry or particular firm is in decline;
cyclical change reflecting national and international economic activity; and, policy changes,
which are really accelerated structural changes,
resulting from direct government action or, for
example, the merger of firms. Technological
change is, therefore, a problem that can confront
the older worker in addition to other changes:

> A change in technology may well add to
> the burden imposed on the adjustment
> mechanism of the labour market by
> other forms of economic change.
> (Hunter, Reid and Boddy, 1970, p. 19)

The cumulative effect of such changes within a local
labour market means that employment prospects for
older workers diminish rapidly even where they
already have marketable skills, or acquire them.

> Of the young trainees, 69.2 per cent
> found work immediately compared with
> 45.0 per cent of the men over forty.
> Although theory suggests that men will
> require to be trained or re-trained in
> mid-life as the skills they learnt when
> young became redundant, it would appear
> that the prospects for men in middle
> age will be bleak unless the prejudices
> of employers towards hiring older men can
> be broken down.
> (Hall and Miller, 1975, p. 92)

Once unemployed, older workers are likely to find themselves subject to age discrimination in their search for re-employment. Jolly, Creigh and Mingay (1980) noted in a recent analysis of age as an element in job advertisements:

> Although the sample of jobs limited to older workers is small, it may be note-worthy that this is the category with the highest proportion of exceptions (35.5 per cent). It may thus be inferred that employers will more readily accept a younger person if the opportunity arises.
> (Jolly, Creigh and Mingay, 1980, p. 30)

Similarly, although resulting from a contrived experimental situation, Rosen and Jerdee (1976) noted a clear pattern of age discrimination in the simulated decision making of 'managers'.

Age discrimination can, at one level, be regarded as a practical manifestation of cultural stereo-types of the old, and of ageing. Slater (1978) has, for example, argued that failures of the age discrimination legislation in the United States are related to the widespread and irrational stereotype of the older worker (11). There is probably something in this because an alternative view suggesting discrimination is little more than a labour market mechanism to handle labour sur-pluses fails to acknowledge that even at times of labour shortage, the older workers' best chances were with the employer who knew their strengths and did not just guess at their weak-nesses.

> Individuals will differ, but there seems little doubt that as a group men begin to show their age by the mid-fifties. An employer will probably be quite happy to continue to employ a man of this age whose abilities he knows. But once that man is out of work, potential new employers will look askance at him, fearful of what his sickness record may be, and of what effort can be expected from him. Where he has a choice, the employer will nearly always take the younger man.
> (Wedderburn, 1965, p. 85)

It is, however, true that in times of labour shortages interest in older workers is likely to go beyond mere tolerance for their continued employment to actual encouragement of it. Nevertheless, as Clark (1963) observed, even that was a process which involved a certain amount of selectivity:

> They usually wished to retain in their own
> department a man for whom they had a
> liking; they would therefore prepare
> his mind gradually for a move, so that
> it could be effected as soon as the
> opportunity came. This in their view
> was often a rather delicate business.
> Some of them said that it might take
> a year, from the time when they first
> began, to convince an older man that
> it would be in his interest to make
> a move. Usually, they thought it was
> a matter of convincing him that the
> greater security of employment would
> compensate for the smaller pay packet.
> (Clark, F., 1963, p. 23)

The 1980s have, however, been a time when technological, structural, cyclical and policy changes have combined to produce a surplus of labour thereby amplifying the traditional problems of industrial senescence. Such changes have enhanced the vulnerability of the older worker by jeopardising existing jobs, and simultaneously, reducing the chances of internal labour mobility as a solution. These are the circumstances that have favoured the implementation of labour reduction mechanisms, such as redundancy and early retirement, in which older workers are prominent. The older worker's employment is not just vulnerable, but increasingly vulnerable, as a result of economic and technological changes and because mechanisms have been developed to facilitate their removal from the labour force and, indeed, the labour market.

Security and insecurity

Late working life has become increasingly insecure for many older workers at a time in their careers when, because of the problems associated with industrial senescence, and discriminatory practices in the external labour market, they give a high value to job security (12).

It has been demonstrated that not all workers have
the same kind of commitment to their employing
organisation (13), but age in relation to commitment has seldom been a specific research focus.
However, there is some evidence to suggest that
age, in reactive terms, does make workers more
security conscious. Guest (1960), for example,
noted in a study of automobile workers:

> Workers also talked about the reasons
> that they would not leave even if they
> had a chance for another job on the
> outside. The most dominant theme in
> this phase of remarks was the desire to
> maintain job security, and to these
> workers seniority was the symbol of
> security. Closely allied to the
> security theme were such factors as
> fear of being too old to get another
> job, fear of being laid off on
> another job, fear of having to start
> up from the bottom, and fear of not
> being able to make as much money.
> (Guest, 1960, p. 323)

Similarly, Beynon and Blackburn (1972) observed
that orientations towards work varied between their
four sub-groups of manual workers:

> ... orientations, we have argued, will
> vary with age and family responsibil-
> ities and so it is significant that
> the frequency with which 'security of
> employment' and 'fringe benefits' were
> quoted increased progressively with
> the age of the respondents, being
> particularly marked among those over
> 50 ... In our society manual workers
> who approach retirement age become
> increasingly vulnerable and this fact
> is clearly demonstrated by the men on
> the night shift.
> (Beynon and Blackburn, 1972, p. 48)

Worries about job loss, per se, are often augmented by the fact that there is, quite literally,
more at stake for the older worker. Even if
replacement employment is gained, seniority is lost
and that might be of extreme importance in the

event of redundancy from the new job. Also, if
workers who are involved in company pension schemes
change jobs, 'portability' problems with pension
entitlement may mean losses that are irredeemable
given the finite period of the working life which
is left.

   Becker (1977) has suggested that, as a result of
the time they have spent in an organisation,
individuals find that 'side bets' have been made,
and future actions are to some extent controlled by
them. Involvement in pension schemes is an example
he uses, but the entrapment of the worker is more
graphically illustrated in the transcript of
Schieber's testimony on the U.S. Military Retirement
System:

> In term of the military system, the question
> was asked awhile ago, what portion of the
> military work force has less than 8 years
> service. In the fiscal year 1982, it was
> 70.4 per cent. But somewhere around that
> 8-year, 10-year break, we apply what some
> people call golden hand-cuffs. We make
> the attractiveness of this retirement
> period so great that people can't leave
> their jobs. They may be miserable in
> their jobs, not productive, but retire-
> ment is such a large part of their
> compensation that they can't turn their
> back on it.
> (Military Retirement System, 1983, p. 152,
> emphasis added)

   Consciousness of what job loss might mean, even if
a replacement is found, arguably underwrites the
emergence, and display, of personal qualities that
are deemed 'virtues' by the employer. Equally, it
is congruent with the higher levels of job satisfaction reported for older workers in comparison with
their younger counterparts (e.g. Glenn and Weaver,
1982; Wright and Hamilton, 1978).

   The rationality of the older workers' fears is
shown in the analysis of the kind of jobs that are
open to them if they are able to gain re-employment
following job loss. Clark (1957a) mentioned that
some older drivers and conductors, on leaving the
London Transport Executive, found work only in jobs
of a more peripheral nature.

27

> We have little information about the jobs
> men enter outside the industry; but the
> records do indicate for what kinds of
> job they are applying. The occupations
> follow the usual pattern of watchmen,
> messengers, temporary postmen, store-
> keepers, caretakers, shop porters,
> office cleaners and office employees.
> It is doubtful whether such jobs would
> attract or be suitable for all men of
> the standing of ex-drivers or ex-
> conductors.
> (Clark, F., 1957a, p. 20)

More recently, Hunt (1978) was able to conclude that
the last job was not identical to the one in which
most of the working life was spent for 31.1 per cent
of males and 34.2 per cent of females in her survey.
The moves were often of a kind too subtle to show in
a broad socio-economic classification but were sus-
pected to be congruent with the kind of job changes
indicated above. Similarly, Parker (1980) found
that:

> A comparison of the details of main life
> jobs with those of jobs held by workers who
> had a different type of work at time of
> interview shows how older workers tend to
> move into a new range of jobs. As compared
> with main life jobs, proportionately more
> post-main life jobs were as junior non-
> manual and unskilled manual workers, and
> proportionately fewer as skilled and semi-
> skilled manual workers. Particular occup-
> ations which were more likely to be post-
> main life work included clerks/cashiers and
> charwomen/cleaners and the industries invol-
> ved were likely to be services and distribut-
> ive trades.
> (Parker, 1980, p. 36)

Following job loss, older workers seeking re-
employment are more likely to face protracted
unemployment or a marginalisation of their employment status. Pyke (1982), echoing Belbin's
(1955) comments some 27 years earlier, concludes
that only older men with strong, marketable
skills have reasonable prospects in retaining,
or regaining, employment. For others, their
weakened position in the labour market

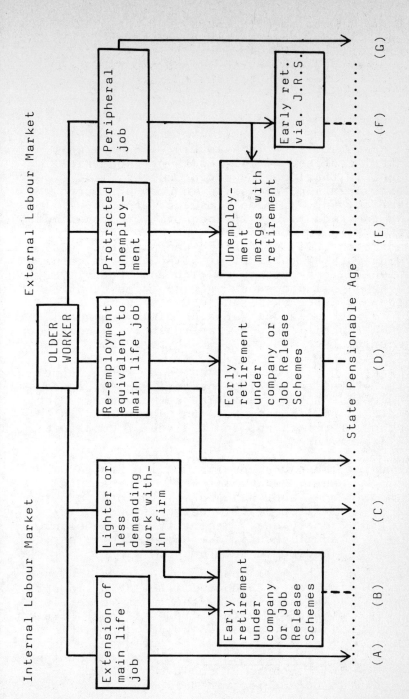

Figure 1.2 Late working life careers

suggests:

> It may be that secure employment for
> older men may only be achieved at the
> cost of a very high trade-off in
> terms of pay and/or other conditions.
> Older men feel constrained to take,
> or stick with, jobs other younger men
> would not stand.
> (Pyke, 1982, p. 48)

The insecurities of late working life are not,
therefore, confined to ill-health or industrial
senescence; the labour-shedding potential of
process innovation, recession-induced workforce
contraction, and skill obsolescence are super-
imposed uncertainties. If insecurity resolves into
job loss, then further uncertainties emerge in the
form of potentially protracted unemployment, or
regaining work at the cost of slippage from core
to peripheral employment (D'Amico and Brown, 1982).
Even if such slippage does not involve a negation of
the older worker's skill and experience, it is
likely to involve a down-grading of pay, general
employment conditions and, particularly, subsequent
job security (Atkinson, 1984; Whyte, 1968).

Late working life careers can be differentiated
in terms of their relative insecurity. As Figure
1.2 indicates, there are varied career paths which
culminate in retirement, not just variations in the
mechanisms of retirement and the age of departure
from a labour force.

Career (A) : The older worker's skills are required
             until reaching the state pensionable
             age, and the capacity to work is not
             limited by ill-health or industrial
             senescence. Seniority, and pension
             entitlements, are gained in the period
             leading to retirement.

Career (C) : With skill-obsolescence, or diminished
             capacity through ill-health or indust-
             rial senescence, the older worker is
             transferred to a 'transitional' (i.e.
             lighter, less-demanding) job within
             the firm. Such a career depends on
             the opportunities that exist, and the
             willingness of employers to deploy
             older workers in this way. Some loss

to current earnings might be involved and the eventual occupational pension, if available, may be reduced but service is continued to the state pensionable age.

Career (B) : Within a firm,career paths (A) and (C) may end short of the state pensionable age with recession-induced labour reductions, or a 'swamping' of transitional work opportunities in the wake of process innovation. Company pension schemes, if available, or the Job Release Scheme, finance the early retirement.

Career (D) : The older worker, following job loss, gains equivalent employment with another organisation. Previous company pension entitlements may be 'frozen' until eventual retirement, or the state pensionable age, and it may be too late to enter the pension scheme of the subsequent employer. Pay levels may be similar, but seniority is lost and the provisions of the Job Release Scheme would not apply until twelve months of continuous full-time employment were completed.

Career (E) : Job loss followed by protracted unemployment. With adoption of recent administrative conventions, unemployment merges with retirement. 'Signing-on', after a year, no longer necessary and higher rate supplementary benefit available. For some, actuarily reduced occupational pensions may be paid on retirement.

Careers (F) and (G) : After job loss in late working life, a peripheral sector job is obtained. Wage levels and general work conditions are likely to be worse than before, and an occupational pension is unlikely to be earned in this employment. If health is maintained, early retirement is possible through the Job Release Scheme, after twelve months of continuous full-time employment. Seniority is lost and the working life may end in unemployment as in career path (E).

The threshold of retirement, therefore, is more diverse than an analysis of retirement trends, or early retirement mechanisms, would suggest. It is not just that there are varied ways of leaving the labour force or indeed the labour market, but the preludes to some form of retirement are quite different in terms of the degree of protection offered the older worker. For some, retirement, at the state pensionable age or earlier, is the culmination of an orderly career in an organisation that conforms with S.D. Clark's (1959) depiction of the implicit 'contract' of late working life. If the firm was large enough (14) and had a complex technical division of labour, it might even have been that reduced work capacity was accommodated. For others, however, late working life could have been an inherently uncertain period where ill-health, senescence, technological and economic changes, singly or in combination, made them increasingly vulnerable.

LATE WORKING LIFE AND FEELINGS ABOUT RETIREMENT

Given that there are many different organisational routes to retirement, one might have expected a plethora of studies linking late working life experiences to feelings about retirement. Strangely, this is not the case. What we do find, however, are studies which acknowledge the salience of occupational factors, but very few which focus on organisational circumstances of occupational practice as they relate to retirement attitudes.

The clearest statement of the relationship between occupational experiences and the subsequent retirement was presented by Friedmann and Havighurst (1977) in a study originally published in 1954. Not only was it recognised that ... 'what retirement means to a person depends partly on what his work has meant to him'(Friedmann and Havighurst, 1977, p. 187), but that the meanings given to work vary according to the occupation of the individual.

The main problem with this research, however, despite its theoretical and empirical value, was that the meaning given to work in specific occupations was presented in a largely atemporal fashion; i.e. the way that meanings might change in the passage through late working life as a response to differing, or changing, employment circumstances was not considered. So, while the constituent occupational studies tell the reader what working as a physician, steelworker or coal miner, for example, means to respondents; no systematic attempt was made to produce anything other than a 'still' of those meanings. Yet, in the study of skilled craftsmen (Friedmann and Havighurst, 1977, pp. 145 - 155) age variations in the meaning given to work were noted though the pattern was far from clear. It was equally noteworthy that the research design did not control for employment circumstances in using a mailed questionnaire, based on a print union nominal roll, and including no analysis of responses on the basis of employing organisation variables. The concluding question appears to recognise this problem:

> How does the particular social situation
> affect the predominant meaning assigned
> to work?
> (Friedmann and Havighurst, 1977, p. 155)

Sometimes 'work' (15) rather than specific 'occupational' characteristics have been considered in explanation of the variation in retirement perspectives. Crawford (1971), for example, underlined the differential views of retirement held by manual and non-manual workers but explained the variance in terms of the relationship between work and non-work roles. So, while the experience of work is accorded significance; it is incorporated in fairly broad terms, and does not focus on employment circumstances of late working life. Hochschild's (1975) development of Crawford's work ultimately adds little in this respect, but suggests 'access to work', a labour market dimension, is salient in patterns of engagement and disengagement. This, in conjunction with 'work satisfaction in middle age' provides a framework for considering possible changes in both variables in the years leading up to retirement. However, the discussion remains at a high level of abstraction in pursuit of disengagement theory arguments.

Occupation has, therefore, had a somewhat idiosyncratic role in retirement research. It has been acknowledged as a useful variable in the understanding of what retirement means to people because it encapsulates much of what they are in terms of self-identity, social position and financial

standing (16). Even so, one could hardly regard
this acknowledgement as universal and often even
where such recognition exists, elements of occupation are analysed (e.g. Jacobson, 1972a, 1972b;
Quinn, 1978) rather than more extensive reviews of
the links between occupation, employment, and
retirement.

Furthermore, it could be suggested that while
occupational characteristics are salient; what also
matters, in the understanding of how retirement is
perceived, is the employment context of occupational
practitioners. For not only do the meanings assig-
ned to work vary according to broad occupational
experiences of practitioners, but also according to
the context in which they are employed.

> Certainly how the individual feels about
> his job has an impact on how he will view
> the prospect of retiring. The important
> point is that this impact does not take
> place in a vacuum but occurs instead in
> the context of the individual's own
> personal situation.
> (Atchley, 1976, p. 28)

Health and family circumstances are part of that
'personal situation', but so also are employment
circumstances. Some members of an occupational
group will have had continuous careers with organisations that make good provisions for workers,
while at work, and in their retirement; in sickness
and in health. Others will have worked for a series
of employers with little commitment on either side;
or for employers who demonstrate little concern for
their employees over and above the immediate
contract of employment. Equally, even in the
context of technological and economic change, some
employers will be both willing and able to provide
secure employment for older workers; others,
through circumstance or inclination, will be less
accommodating. Changes in the technological and
economic environment are mediated through individual
employers.

The nature of the employing organisation and the
responses that are made in terms of manpower figures
and manpower policy, however, have been even less
in evidence in retirement research than occupational
characteristics.

The value of considering specific employment contexts can be seen in Wood's (1980) study of the 'Northern Process Company'. Although the focus is on what redundancies through early retirement mean to 'surviving' managers, rather than those who have left, the ambience created by the policy of handling redundancies ... 'in a way designed to result in the minimum amount of fuss' (Wood, 1980, p. 802) can be seen to engender certain patterns of self-appraisal in the late working life of survivors. A belief in personal immunity from the changes that de-emphasised structural vulnerability appeared to be the most pervasive coping strategy.

> Most evaluated the early retirements
> within individualistic terms, and
> hence judged the retirers to be
> 'deserving of their fate' or to be
> benefiting from leaving the firm.
> (Wood, 1980, p. 801)

> Only one person reported feeling
> currently more insecure about the
> possibility of losing his job than
> when he first joined the firm ...
> (Wood, 1980, p. 798)

For present purposes, the importance of this study is the light it throws on the circumstances of late working life and, in particular, the interrelation of company history, company policy, and worker morale. Doubtless a much different story would have emerged in other organisations where the firm was regarded more suspiciously by employees, and where provision for those retired early was less generous.

Equally, perceptions of retirement and life in retirement are differentially influenced by the employing organisation; its relationship to local communities, and the worker's personal biography within that organisation are of relevance. Lehr and Dreher hint at the significance of the employing organisation:

> Workers who were members of the company
> with the most modern equipment and also
> the most pleasant social atmosphere,
> judged the situation most positively,
> but their attitudes toward retirement
> were most negative ...
> (Havighurst et al, 1969, p. 127)

It is Thomae (in Havighurst et al, 1969) though, who reveals most about the study from which this observation was made. Steelworkers from three different mills were interviewed and, although occupation was held constant, differences in perception of, and response to, retirement were noted. Though only brief summaries of mill differences were presented, reported variations include technology, mill history and social climate.

Retired workers from one mill were more likely to have positive attitudes to retirement, express greater satisfaction immediately after retirement and at the point of interview; and have greater feelings of security, than those who were similarly ex-steel workers but who were retirees from different mills. The way that different employment contexts influenced such orientations was not reported by Thomae who, consistent with the theme of the work in which this report appears, was more concerned to address the implications of the study for disengagement theory. The insights offered by this study of steelworkers are profound, yet they appear to be largely unheeded as guides to subsequent research.

SUMMARY

Retirement can be regarded as a formal societal response to the problem of older workers' weak labour market position. Its emergence, in theory at least, supplanted the slide into unemployability that had previously accompanied old age. Given recognition of retirement as part of the life path, most older people ceased competing for work at the point when they became eligible for an alternative source of income - the age at which state pensions were payable. However, the fact that state pensions are paid at fixed chronological ages creates a further problem. The older workers' diminishing power in the labour market must coincide with this pensionable age. In practice, though, such an occurrence could only be fortuitous. Some would find continued employment, or re-employment, problematic before the state pensionable age. Others, with good health and a strong demand for their skills, might have easily worked on past this age.

At present, decreased economic activity rates, and
the incidence of long-term unemployment among older
people, suggests a general weakening in their labour
market position well before the state pensionable
age. Within this general state of affairs, though,
there are going to be variations in older workers'
experiences, with much of this variation resulting
from the particular characteristics of employing
organisations.

It would not seem unreasonable to suppose that the
experiences of late working life will influence the
way that retirement is perceived. Indeed, one could
formulate this as an explicit hypothesis: employment circumstances in late working life will be a
determinant of perspectives on retirement (17).

Given the points raised in this chapter's broadly-
based review of older worker vulnerability, it would
be possible to propose several areas, and types, of
research to test the hypothesis. We do not, for
example, know much about perspectives on retirement
from a position of late working life unemployment.
Equally, longitudinal studies through late working
life and into retirement would be useful for an
understanding of how perspectives alter.

The study presented in the chapters which follow
is necessarily limited in its scope, and concentrates
only on the re-negotiation of the work role in later
life considering the circumstances of employing
organisations as they relate to varying possibilities
for deployment and redeployment of older men. As
such it is primarily a contribution to our understanding of the salience of late working life.

NOTES

(1)   With profound irony, unemployed workers are
       categorised as economically active.
(2)   Subsequently made country-wide.
(3)   Employment Gazette (April 1980) cites an NOP
       survey for the Department of Employment in
       which it was revealed that 58 per cent of
       Job Release Scheme applicants were in receipt
       of an occupational pension.
(4)   The Job Release Scheme guidelines (Department
       of Employment, 1981; 1984) state different
       rates of allowance for those with income from

an occupational pension scheme, but notes
that receipt of an occupational pension will
not affect eligibility for the allowance.

(5)   The Job Release Scheme guidelines (Department
of Employment, 1981; 1984) indicate that
four weeks notice are required of a person in
receipt of an allowance wishing to leave the
scheme.

(6)   This distorts recent figures for long-term
unemployment. For example, the proportion of
unemployed men, aged 55 years and over, who
had been out of work for more than a year
actually fell between January 1983 and January
1984 (Employment Gazette, February 1984,
Table 2.5, p. S33). Footnotes to the table
acknowledge that this is a statistical arti-
fact rather than a change in the 'real'
situation. Equally, it is these changes in
the classification of older unemployed men,
rather than markedly different re-employment
prospects, that explains the strangely
different 'duration of unemployment' profile
of unemployed men aged over 60 years as
compared with those aged 55-59 years (Social
Trends, 1986, Table 4.22, p. 73).

(7)   For a diagrammatic representation of the
routes to retirement see Parker (1980, Fig.
3, p. 10).

(8)   It is estimated that, at current rates of
benefit, the cost of a reduction in male
retirement age from 65 to 60 years - thus
making 60 years the retirement age for both
men and women - would be in the order of
£2,000 million (T.U.C., circa 1981, paragraph 6, p. 6). While there are some
800,000 employed men between the ages of 60
and 65 years, even generous estimates
suggest that only two-thirds of the jobs
vacated could immediately be filled by the
unemployed (T.U.C., circa 1981, paragraph
39, p. 12).

(9)   For further discussion, see T.U.C. (circa
1981) and Walker (1982).

(10) In the United States the debate about fixed
retirement ages is further advanced with
amendments to the Age Discrimination in
Employment Act (1967) in 1978 to prohibit
mandatory retirement in the private sector
before age 70 years, and abolish mandatory
retirement from Federal employing agencies,

(see Sykes, 1982). In part, this was an acknowledgement of the possible negative effects of compulsory retirement on older workers, but fiscal considerations were highly salient to the changes, (see Litras, 1979).

(11)   For a review of literature on the behaviour of older workers, and organisational foibles in relation to older workers, see Doering, Rhodes, and Schuster (1983).

(12)   For evidence of increasing 'viscosity' in job mobility with age, see General Household Survey 1980 (1982, Table 5.30, p. 114).

(13)   See, for example, Gouldner's discussion of cosmopolitans and locals (in Grusky and Miller, 1970, pp. 477-482); and Becker's account of teacher's careers (Becker, 1977, pp. 165-175).

(14)   In his discussion of labour market theory, Kreckel (1980) cautions that the notion of internal labour markets is closely associated with big manufacturing industries and, in detail, is not well adapted to other types of organisation. He concedes, however, that differentiation between core and fringe jobs is a model set for the entire labour market.

(15)   Work is a somewhat broader concept than occupation although there is overlap in colloquial usage, and in the literature. Work, for example, includes not only what is done in pursuit of an occupation, but can be thought to include non-market activity. Importantly, both can be distinguished from employment which would appear to be the salient concept here (see Jahoda, 1982).

(16)   For discussion of the relationship between work, and social identity see, Jahoda (1982); Marsden and Duff (1975); and Fraser (1969).

(17)   In the Ph.D. research on which this book is based, there was a more broadly-stated hypothesis on the relation between late working life and life in retirement. This book, with a less extensive remit, concentrates heavily on late working life experiences and considers how they relate to perspectives on retirement. Readers interested in the broader relationship between late working life and the early stages of retirement are requested to refer to the thesis (Lyon, 1985).

39

2 Stoneywood Mill

As older workers approach retirement, they do so
within a particular organisational framework. What
happens in that organisation will have an important
influence on late working lives. That much is
certain.

   Organisations with a stable structure and technology will not confront older employees with circumstances that invalidate their experience.
Conversely, in organisations where structural and
technological changes are in progress, older workers
are likely to be much more vulnerable. In addition
to vulnerability arising from a changed demand for
specific skills, or from workers becoming super-
numerary, there is the possibility of industrial
senescence and poor health. Whatever form the
vulnerability takes, the effect on the older worker
is, arguably, mediated through two further dimensions
of the employing organisation. First, there is what
might be termed the style of employer-employee
relations. If employers acknowledge a commitment
to the continued employment of older workers, then
the prospect of redundancy or premature retirement
is lessened. Second, even if such a commitment is
clear, organisations vary in the number and range of
suitable jobs to which older workers could be

redeployed.

In this chapter, something of the history and structure of Stoneywood Mill is presented. As a context for late working life it had two important attributes - a paternalistic style of management and division of labour complex enough to absorb older workers displaced by failing health, industrial senescence and reorganisation. Things were, however, changing.

PATERNALISM AND THE DONSIDE DYNASTY

Stoneywood Mill has a pedigree that began in the earliest stages of the Industrial Revolution with the replacement of the old land-based social order. The period from 1770 is a time scale that has not only seen the physical growth and technological development of the mill, but also the establishment of a taken-for-granted frame of reference in the relations between employers and employees. That framework is essentially paternalistic.

Essentially, paternalism is a style of workplace relations in which the employer's power is handled in a manner supposedly (1) resembling that of the patriarch in a family setting. As Abercrombie and Hill (1976) point out, paternalism had a functional appeal in the early stages of industrialisation because it offered a solution to the mismatch between the skills and discipline of the workforce, and the requirements of the new mode of production. To a large extent, paternalism may be seen as a transitional control strategy providing a bridge between new and old social leaders; between new and old modes of production. Arguably, it was eclispsed by more narrowly defined and more formal contractual relations between employers and employees (Bendix, 1963; Abercrombie and Hill, 1976).

However, just as it was not always the case that employers saw paternalism as a real (2) guide to labour management practice; its demise was not uniform. Lane and Roberts (1971), and Martin and Fryer (1973) have demonstrated its modified survival in two family firms until very recent times; even if they were primarily concerned with the conditions under which that frame of reference collapsed.

41

> Management at Casterton Mills thus
> continued to operate within the
> framework of paternalistic capitalism
> until the 1960s, with only marginal
> adaptations to meet new circum-
> stances. Workers at Casterton
> Mills did the same; their
> attitudes were, to a large extent,
> complementary to those of manage-
> ment. Casterton Mills workers
> believed in loyalty, obedience,
> and the need to accept managerial
> authority; they respected the
> virtues which helped to sustain
> paternalistic capitalism.
> (Martin and Fryer, 1973, p. 72)

From both studies, it appears that justification
for the epithet of paternalism rests on identification of the following features. First, there is a
broadly-based interpretation of the employer-
employee relationship. That is, employer interest
in workers' lives which goes ... 'beyond the
appropriation of their labour' (Lane and Roberts,
1973, p. 228). Second, the employer's authority is
largely unchallenged, there being widespread
deference on the part of employees. Third, long
service and loyalty are recognised as important by
both employers and employees.

It is in relation to these points that Stoneywood
Mill is characterised as a paternalistic place of
employment. The sustained paternalism (3) was, in
part, the product of dynastic control. Following
a series of ownership, and part-ownership, changes
in its first thirty years, the mill was to develop
in the hands of the Pirie family for the next 122
years (4) and, while amalgamation in 1922 with
Wiggins Teape Ltd. served to diffuse control, the
family maintained a presence in the post-war years
that form part of the working lives of older and
retired mill employees interviewed for this study.

Dynastic control was an important factor because
it underwrote, and gave continuity to, a particular
kind of relationship between the mill and the local
community. Although the mill's workforce expanded
from some 30 workers in 1820 (Cruickshank, 1946)
to 1500 in 1879 (Bartlett, 1980), and associated
works were established in Aberdeen (5), Stoneywood

remained the centrepiece of the Pirie empire. Not
only was it the family 'seat', but the position was
consolidated with acquisition of much of the
surrounding land (Morgan, P., 1886). The Piries
thus established a land base which replicated that
of the old Lairds of Stoneywood and, occupying a
similar role, adopted a pattern of relations with
their workforce and the adjacent community that
echoed the old order.

   Abercrombie and Hill (1976) suggest that the
inadequate infrastructure of industrialisation gave
employers the opportunity to increase their control
through the provision of housing, schooling and
other facilities for their workers. In this vein,
Pirie's instituted a works library as early as 1849
which was open to all company employees, 'tradesmen
and labourers employed at the works' (Pirie and
Sons, 1871), and persons residing in the neighbour-
hood. Equally, a school was erected and maintained
to serve the needs of employees' families. It
lasted from 1865 to 1880 after which it became the
Works Hall used as a centre for several village
social activities (Cruickshank, 1934). Even on the
occasion of the mill's 150th. anniversary, the
Pirie's involvement with the local infrastructure
was still evident.

> ... Messrs. Pirie have recently gifted
> 19 acres of ground to the Aberdeen
> District Committee for the erection of
> dwelling houses at Stoneywood under
> the housing scheme. The building of
> the first instalment of 62 four-roomed
> cottages will commence next month.
> (Aberdeen Daily Journal, 14 August 1920)

   Pirie family members differed in style, but more
in terms of variations on a theme than any outright
rejection of the firm's paternalistic presence in
the community. One of the more interesting members
of the family, from the paternalism point of view,
was Francis Logie Pirie (1841 - 1915). His public
addresses on employer-employee relations clearly
demonstrate the paternalistic philosophy. His
lecture on 'Co-operation in production' given at
Stoneywood Church Hall in aid of the church building
fund, made explicit reference to the idealised
family model of work relations prior to industrialisation.

The connection then between the employer
and the workmen was of the closest.
Very often the workmen lodged with their
employers, fed at the same table, and
formed part of the same family. When a
workman married and established a home
of his own, the employer still maintained
the same kindly interest in the fortunes
of himself and his family. In the work-
room, employer and workman could be
seen at work side by side - the latter,
though rewarded only with a weekly wage,
as interested in the success of the
venture as the former.
(Pirie, F.L., 1884, p. 17)

Bemoaning the loss of such a close relationship
with the development of large industrial enterprises,
he advocated a form of industrial partnership to
foster equal interest in the venture. In a manner
reminiscent of Frederick Taylor (Taylor, 1967),
though, he saw the moral character of workmen as a
major obstacle. Although he appears to have
reconciled himself to the fact that close adherence
to the paternalism of the small-scale enterprise
was no longer possible; he did, apparently (6)
still work within the basic conventions of
paternalism.

He took a great interest in the works,
and every time he came north showed
his practical concern in the welfare
of the employees by calling at many
of their houses. Once they got Mr.
Logie Pirie's favour they never
lost it; he was loyal to them in
every way.
(Aberdeen Daily Journal, 15 May 1915)

Although the mill was amalgamated with Wiggins
Teape Ltd. in 1922, the name Alexander Pirie and
Sons was used into the 1960s, and the Pirie family
maintained a boardroom presence into the post-war
years (Morgan, D., 1983).

We always said that when Wiggins ...
[the change of name in the 1960s] ...
came in that we didn't work for
Wiggins. We were Pirie's ... we old
ones - it might be Wiggins Teape
or BAT - we're all Pirie's. You

hear people **squealing** about working
for this family - they were this or
that - but we were proud.
(Retired employee)

The style of employer-employee relations became
firmly entrenched, with successive generations of
mill workers and mill officials acknowledging the
model, in spite of changing industrial and infra-
structural conditions. MacKenzie's review of the
Aberdeen paper industry in 1953 noted the stability
of employment practices.

> Because of traditional ties between the
> mills and the communities in which they
> are located, there is a large element
> of mutual goodwill between management
> and workers. At Culter, Woodside,
> Mugiemoss and Stoneywood, there live
> families whose connexions with the
> paper mill started before the present
> century began. Managements have
> encouraged the loyalty of their
> workers by considerable expenditure
> on social amenities for the community,
> such as the purchase of sports grounds,
> recreation halls, and the promotion
> of social clubs, and at least two
> benefit and pension schemes are in
> operation.
> (MacKenzie, 1953, p. 279)

Changes occurred but were largely absorbed within
the paternalistic framework. In the post-war period,
the mill's labour demands caused an extension of the
traditional catchment area into the northern part
of Aberdeen. This brought the possibility of new
perspectives on the employer-employee relationship.
The period could well have signalled the collapse
of paternalism.

> You can't consider them a bad firm.
> They've been a good firm for the
> whole community really, I would say.
> You get criticisms, you get criticisms
> everywhere though. Old-time manage-
> ment used to employ fathers, sons,
> grandsons, sisters and mothers. They
> were all part of the mill. It was
> more like a family concern, you know,
> at Stoneywood, until they started

opening it up with strangers coming in,
change of management, and so on. You
know, they didn't seem to care that much
for you. Obviously it wasn't the same ...
each one knew another one, knew his
father, and so on, you know ... local.
Whereas all of us, what I term outsiders,
coming into the mill started to change
things.

When did the strangers start coming in?

I would say about the 1950's, when I
started. OK, there were a lot of
outsiders in a sense but I'm speaking
about people who lived in the town.
Myself, when I started there first,
I can remember it was all local people
and they'd kind of look at you strange
as though you were something from
another planet. Oh, they're alright,
like everything else, you get on with
people.
(Worker, aged 57 years)

   Although there was some dilution in traditional
recruitment patterns, there was accommodation of
these changes as there had earlier been for trade
unions (7). Among the current and retired employees
interviewed, there was evidence of a wider catchment
area but, by present day commuting standards, these
men lived close to the mill. Taking both groups of
workers, 55.2 per cent lived in the neighbouring
villages of Stoneywood, Bucksburn and Dyce while
virtually all the remainder lived in the northern
part of Aberdeen. On the basis of direct distances
from the mill, 82.8 per cent lived within a 2.5
mile radius.

   While changes had undoubtedly occurred, it was
clear that mill management still took a broad view
of their role in the immediate community; and in
workers' welfare. In 1979, when the local church
celebrated its centenary, secular activities
included a picnic in Polo Park with Stoneywood
Works Band in attendance (8) (Evening Express,
1 September 1979). Each year the firm plays a
significant role in the local gala week with an
open night at the mill and a mill pensioners' lunch
being part of the traditional range of events
(Wiggins Teape (UK), Summer 1981).

The mill's Sports and Social Club demonstrates something of the complex relationship implied by industrial paternalism. In 1974 new club premises were opened as a result of co-operation between owners and workers. The £35,000 needed for the project was raised by a workers' committee (9) at the mill, and much of the actual building work was undertaken by employees in their spare time. The firm showed more than token acknowledgement of the term 'retired employee' in its establishment of a Senior Citizens' section to the club in 1981. Although mill management reacted to representations made by retired workers and did not initiate the idea, they provided support. Reaction rather than initiation is consistent with the paternalism espoused by Francis Logie Pirie (Pirie, F.L., 1884; 1889) with its emphasis on the guided participation of workers rather than simple donation by owners.

Over the years, Stoneywood Mill built a reputation for being a stable employer; a provider of secure jobs. This reputation was particularly important in the stark pre-war years when many of the now-retired men were young and faced with the prospect of increasing domestic commitments.

> Well, you see, down at Stoneywood at
> that particular time it was the elite.
> People used to queue up to get a job
> at Stoneywood. If you got a job at
> Stoneywood you were considered very,
> very lucky because it was steady, and
> it wasn't too bad a place to work.
> (Retired employee)

> I had a couple of years on a butcher's
> bike, you see. I was looking for a
> job all the time I was working at the
> other job, you see. So, every week I
> was down to see if I could get a job
> at the mill, and once I did get the
> job, I was in there and that was that -
> the same as my father and them before
> me, you see. They just said, "Well, go
> down the mill and it's a job for life."
> (Worker, aged 61 years)

Table 2.1

Mill sample: age on entry

	Retired men		Current workers		All men	
	No.	Per cent	No.	Per cent	No.	Per cent
14-20 years	17	41.5	5	29.4	22	37.9
21-30 years	11	26.8	5	29.4	16	27.6
31-40 years	5	12.2	2	11.8	7	12.1
41-50 years	4	9.8	3	17.7	7	12.1
51-60 years	4	9.8	2	11.8	6	10.3
61 + years	0	0	0	0	0	0
Totals	41	100.1	17	100.1	58	100.0

The Aberdeen labour market was not particularly
strong, in terms of diversity or demand, until the
advent of oil exploration and its ancillary
activities. Security continued to be important in
the post-war decades, and never really faltered for
men who were, by the 1970s, unable or unwilling to
capitalise on the changing market situation.

> No, I was quite happy. There was quite
> a few lads at one time of day - they had
> just a few years with us - left to go to
> the building trade and things of that
> sort. I always said, "How long will
> that last? The paper trade - there'll
> always be paper to make so I'd rather
> stick here with maybe a wee bit less
> money." But there was always a few ...
> (Retired employee)

Exploitation of new labour market opportunities
seems largely to have been the province of young,
and less entrenched (10), paperworkers. For the
rest, the mill was a long-term employer.

> I think that if we look at all the
> statistics we've turned out in this
> mill over the last ten, fifteen or
> twenty years, they've all revealed
> the major turnover being in the age
> group of under 25 years with less
> than 2 years' service. That's always

the big one. I think once they've
passed the 2 to 3 years service, and
they're that bit older - into their
thirties - they're going to stay
with you until they retire.

Do you still see this as true for the
men who are thirty now?

I think so. Not necessarily for the
same reasons, however, but I think its
going to be proven. We did a survey,
not so very long ago. It followed a
massive advert in the Press and Journal
where we thanked approximately 200
people for service over 25 years.
Then, a quick breakdown revealed almost
400 people - almost fifty per cent of
the complement - had done 20 years.
That's quite mind blowing. So there's
obviously not the turnover; the turnover's down in the younger age group.
(Company manager)

Table 2.2

Mill sample: years of service completed at
retirement or interview

	Retired men		Current workers		All men	
	No.	Per cent	No.	Per cent	No.	Per cent
10 years or less	3	7.3	2	11.8	5	8.6
11-20 years	2	4.9	3	17.7	5	8.6
21-30 years	8	19.5	4	23.5	12	20.7
31-40 years	12	29.3	4	23.5	16	27.6
41-50 years	12	29.3	4	23.5	16	27.6
51 years	4	9.8	0	0	4	6.9
Totals	41	100.1	17	100.1	58	100.0

The men in the samples had impressive service
records with the mill. Over two-thirds of those
who had completed their careers had been at
Stoneywood for 31 years or more, as had just under
half of the older workers at the time of interview.

Although years of service do not, in themselves,
give an unambiguous measure of loyalty, they did
appear to be mutually acknowledged as an important
feature of the employer-employee relationship.
Long service was the trigger for an elaborate system
of recognition ceremonies involving gifts at the 15
and 35 year points. With the latter came membership
of the 35 Year Club and annual wining and dining at
a local hotel. Service became part of the
employee's frame of reference as well:

> Did you want to retire at 63 years?
>
> No, I'll be honest. The wife'll tell
> you. I took a long time to make up
> my mind. I was wanting to do the
> 50 years. I was going to be proud
> of my 50 years.
> (Retired employee)

It would, however, be unrealistic to suppose that
the general economic changes of the last few years,
and the difficulties of the paper industry over
the last 15 years, allowed mill management an
untroubled relationship with employees. Process
innovation and demanning caused problems for
workers and owners alike, but the paternalistic
ethos served to blunt some of the more traumatic
effects.

PRODUCT MARKET PROBLEMS AND MANAGEMENT RESPONSE

The paper industry has been one of the less-
publicised victims of entrapment between high
domestic production costs and strengthening
international competition. The problems
encircling the industry have been closing for over
two decades (Paper Centenary Issue, 1979), but
over the last ten to fifteen years the problems
have become markedly worse.

Energy costs have risen in the UK, but overseas
competitors have either had situational advantages,
such as hydro-electric power, or beneficial cost
arrangements ranging from direct subsidisation to
energy cost reductions for process use (SOGAT,
1981). The net result was a high burden even in
relation to EEC competitors (Paper, 4 October 1982)
let alone those in Scandinavia and North America
with their 'double squeeze' advantage on woodpulp

(11). The UK recession of the last five years or so
added a new range of difficulties to an already
weakened industry.

Few industries could have presented annual
reviews with such singularly unhappy titles: 'The
paper industry proves its resilience' (Paper Review
of the Year, 1975); 'UK viable, but ...' (Paper
Review of the Year, 1977); 'It was a poor year for
most and disastrous for some' (Paper Review of the
Year, 1981); 'An unhappy chapter for UK papermakers' (Paper Review of the Year, 1982); and
'Gloom closes in again' (Paper Review of the Year,
1983). Mill closures, machine shutdowns, and
redundancies have been commonplace since the early
1970s with noticeable blackspots at either end of
the decade, and a steady sequence of mill and
machine closure in the intervening period (Paper
Review of the Year, 1983).

The British Paper and Board Industry Federation
reported (12) a net 29 per cent reduction in the
UK labour force for the Paper and Board Making
sector over the period 1970 to 1979. In member
mills of the British Paper and Board Industry
Federation, 20,000 jobs were lost between November
1977 and January 1983 (Paper, 24 January 1983).

Local mills had not been immune to these national
trends. The most dramatic expression of problems
in the industry was the closure of Culter Paper
Mill in the western suburbs of Aberdeen. Closure
was attributed to the unprofitability of its coated
paper products - the mainstay of the mill - in
spite of its 'improved quality and increased
productivity' (Paper Review of the Year, 1981,
p. 27). The 230 year old mill announced its
intention to close in November 1980 following a
period of three and four day working started in the
beginning of that year. Over 1980 the workforce
dwindled from 410 to a final 320 who were declared
redundant. Culter Mill closed in February 1981.
A mile from Stoneywood, Mugiemoss Mill closed its
making machine for bag and wrapping grade paper
with a loss of 118 jobs (Paper Review of the Year,
1982). Industrial difficulties were painfully
apparent at local level.

Stoneywood, as part of the Wiggins Teape group,
fared better than most with its long standing

51

commitment to capital investment for the making of specialised products. As far back as 1967, a £1 million development of Stoneywood was announced (Press and Journal, 1 December 1967). Emphasis was placed on the fact that these developments would put the mill in the 'quality class' of coated papers with application to a wide and rising market. In 1974, a further investment programme was announced (Press and Journal, 21 March 1974). This was to increase production of specialist casting paper used in the manufacture of PVC and polyurethane materials. Again, the focus was on 'trading up' production to more specialised, and more difficult to make, grades of paper with a correspondingly reduced dependance on lower grades more economically produced in Canada and Scandinavia.

It was quite clear, though, that increased employment was not to be a corollary of these investment programmes. In fact, as a result of process innovation, jobs started to be lost. At the time of the 1967 programme, 1500 people were employed at the mill. By 1981, only 810 were working there. In January 1981, with local attention focussed on the collapse of Culter Mill, Wiggins Teape were anxious to assure the press (Press and Journal, 16 January 1981) that while jobs were still being lost at Stoneywood, cutbacks were to be achieved through natural wastage and voluntary early retirement. Technological change had staved off the prospect of redundancies, but had made an increasing number of jobs redundant. In the paper industry it would seem that demanning, in one form or another, was a consequence of both failure and survival.

> We've become very much involved with
> technical changes in paper making.
> The industry, formerly quite highly
> labour-intensive, has moved to a
> very capital-intensive industry now.
> The computerised paper machines, the
> overhead tackle and equipment, the
> hydraulics, pneumatically powered
> tools and machines ... it's becoming
> a wee bit depersonalised. I worked
> on the production lines when we had,
> possibly, 4 and 5 members of machine
> crews, that decreased to 3 members,
> and so on. You know, I don't know
> what the future holds. Possibly

we'll have one person who controls 4 or
5 paper making machines at a console;
then that really is the end of the line
as regards employment in the paper
industry.
(Company manager)

To some extent, workers displaced as a result of
process innovation were absorbed by the mill's
complex technical division of labour. Figure 2.1
shows that while the core activity of the mill was
paper manufacture, not all workers were directly
employed in production. The making process was
serviced by a number of tradesmen, and a variety of
ancillary personnel. Furthermore, paper production
did not generate large numbers of men performing
near-identical work tasks even when they were
employed in the manufacturing process. There was,
rather, considerable fragmentation of work
depending on location - raw materials handling,
preparation, making, finishing and dispatch.

The diversity of occupational roles, and the
relatively small numbers of men engaged in
particular functions, afforded the firm opportunities for handling workforce reductions on an
individual, or small numbers, basis. This diversity
meant that, in theory, there was capacity within
the organisation for the redeployment of workers.
However, alternative work opportunities were, in
relative terms, a scarce resource given economic
pressures that simultaneously demanded high levels
of capital investment, and discouraged the hoarding
of labour. Such opportunities were, in fact,
decreasing at a time when the need for redeployment
was becoming greater. Older workers were particularly vulnerable in this 'double bind'.

Mill management handled the problems as best they
could. Essentially, there were two strategies.
Redeployment, although increasingly difficult, was
used widely to extend the working lives of older
men. This had been a traditional response given
the paternalistic ethos but had, in the past, been
easier because the capacity was there, and demand
was generated primarily by cases of poor health,
injury or industrial senescence. Even when the
supply of ancillary jobs diminished, and the demand
for redeployment from the making process increased,
management attempted to pursue this policy where

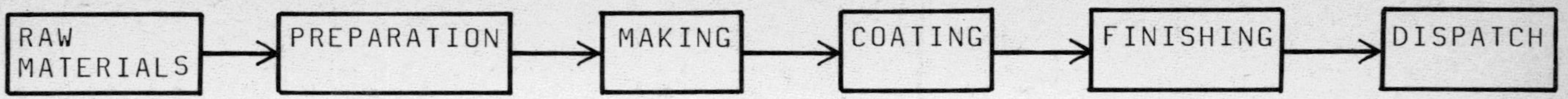

RAW MATERIALS → PREPARATION → MAKING → COATING → FINISHING → DISPATCH

Process roles

Pulperman/Slusher	Machinemen	Cuttermen
Beaterman	Backsiders	Cranemen
Breakerman	Embosserman	Transporting
Rag Boilerman	Film Casting	
	Colour Saturator	

Trade roles

Painting
Welding
Electrician
Joiner
Engraver
Instrument Mechanic
Engineering Machinists
Engineering Fitters

Ancillary roles

Cleaning
Labelling
Printing
Messenger
Outside Squad
Quality Control (*)
Storesmen

(*) Although primarily a white collar
     field, some manual grade workers
     used.

Figure 2.1 Diagrammatic representation of the paper-making process
            with associated process, trade and ancillary occupational
            roles

possible.

> I'll give them credit, there haven't
> been redundancies. The jobs have
> been redundant, but they've employed
> all the people and given them
> different jobs. OK, the people moan
> and groan, but at least they're
> working. They're getting up in the
> morning, and they've a job to go to,
> and they've a wage to lift on a
> Wednesday. I understand industry
> has to change, I know that. The
> industry was overmanned, totally
> overmanned, and the new technology,
> before you catch up there's something
> else coming out, something new
> coming out. So you've got to be on
> your toes, you can't be complacent.
> If you're complacent you're out of
> business, it's as simple as that.
> (Worker, aged 57 years)

However, hindered by labour turnover patterns,
and the supply and demand characteristics of
ancillary posts, management embarked on a second
strategy - 'creaming off' older workers through
early retirements. Redundancies would have
shattered the shared frame of reference (Martin and
Fryer, 1973), but early retirement initiatives by
management, while clearly a form of 'disguised
redundancy' (Ward, S., 1979), could be reconciled
with paternalistic traditions without tortuous
logic.

Solutions available to other industries at other
times, such as the compulsory retirement of men
over 65 years (Rothwell and Zegveld, 1979), were
inappropriate. Management had to ensure a higher
level of retirement among workers before they
reached the state pensionable age.

> The massive service levels that were
> accrued here, of 50 or 51 years, will
> not be possible, for the simple
> reason of the school leaving age and,
> of course, the big change in retire-
> ment. I am going to stick my neck out
> here and say that, in the next two or
> three years, I doubt there will be
> anyone in this place over 60 years

of age.
(Company manager)

Their early retirement policy, financed using
provisions in the existing company pension scheme,
served several discrete but congruent purposes. It
allowed for selective reductions of overall manning
levels in particular departments or functions. It
was a way of handling labour surpluses created by
process innovation and, finally, it allowed a
reduction of workers with impaired health who would
otherwise have expected, and normally received,
sheltered employment to their sixty-fifth
birthdays.

> I have recently been involved with an
> employee who's been off work for a
> long time, and it's very unlikely
> he'll come back to work ... through
> major surgery ... and the fact that
> the only suitable work would be
> light work. We just don't have
> light work now. He will very
> probably have to retire. We're
> both disappointed, and I know for a
> fact that it's not money that's the
> main problem here. He wants to do his
> 8 to 5, and that's it.
> (Company manager)

Early retirement, then, became the major
strategy, overshadowing redeployment. The former
was seen by management, and some workers, to
represent a satisfactory resolution of contradictions between the 'job for life' perception of
employment contracts, and the harsh realities of
the paper industry in the 1970s and 1980s.
However, as shown in Chapter 3, many workers found
the truncation of their working lives disconcerting
having expected redeployment to alternative jobs
as they approached the state pensionable age.

NOTES

(1)   Joyce (1980, p. 136) notes that it was ...
        'this personal embodiment in the family,
        or the family head, that gave paternalism
        its cutting edge.'
(2)   Bendix (1963) comments that the model was
        variously used by those who sought to

eulogise the passing order of decayed
feudalism, and by those extolling the best
practices of the new industrial order; while
it was clearly not descriptive of most
relationships in either. He argues though,
that the paternalism had a wide symbolic
value even if it moulded the practices of
only a few.

(3)   For discussion of local labour market features
        that help sustain industrial paternalism,
        see Norris (1978).

(4)   Bartlett (1980) reports that even when the
        company 'went public' in the latter half of
        the nineteenth century, the family maint-
        ained control of the firm. Between 1898
        and 1914, six of the ten directors were
        Piries and a further two were promotions
        to the board ... 'because of their
        faithful service' (p. 20).

(5)   For a history of the envelope-making works,
        see Morgan, D. (1983).

(6)   It is, perhaps, appropriate to assume a
        level of deference on the part of the local
        press; particularly as the quotation is
        from a 'personal appreciation' at the time
        of F.L. Pirie's death.

(7)   Buckley (1955) describes a bitter strike in
        1889 where paper workers were asking for a
        68 hour week. This developed into a lock-
        out at Stoneywood, and the workers event-
        ually returned on the employer's terms.
        Diack (1939), rather optimistically,
        describes this as a 'draw', and records
        that the union - the Paper Workers' Union -
        had gained a negotiating position by the
        1930s.

(8)   Note similarity with the situation described
        by Dennis, Henriques and Slaughter (1969,
        p. 120).

(9)   There is reference to a workers' committee
        controlling use of a hall for entertain-
        ments and meetings as far back as 1901
        (Aberdeen Daily Journal, 23 August 1901).

(10)   Becker (1977, pp. 261 - 273) uses a 'side
        bet' analogy in his discussion of commit-
        ment. Individuals may wish to leave an
        organisation, but find their freedom of
        action limited by factors such as their
        stake in occupational pension schemes;
        and the fact that their involvement with

one organisation has made them unsuitable for others.

(11)   SOGAT (1981, p. 3) identifies a 'double squeeze' problem for the industry. Overseas competitors often have access to woodpulp which they can exploit to full advantage in their own processing industry, and can increase the price of woodpulp for British paper makers without increasing the price of the paper they export to Britain.

(12)   Figures from British Paper and Board Industry Federation (Industrial Relations Division) mimeo, dated 8 March 1982.

3 Late working life at the mill

INTRODUCTION

The mill's history, and its technological changes,
formed a context for late working life. This period,
foreshadowing retirement, was inherently uncertain.
At 54 years there was, for some, the prospect of
another 11 years of work. For others, the time for
retirement was closer; often much closer than they
realised. Against the possibility of a 'full term'
of employment was set the possibility of health
problems, and the likelihood that changes related to
recession and/or new technology would cause
demanning. While, in essence, such ambiguities
faced all workers, they were particularly prominent
for the older man.

   Currently employed older workers were asked if
they thought they would be able to carry on with
their present job until they reached 65 years. As
Table 3.1 shows, only a minority were explicitly
pessimistic.

   I doubt if anyone will be allowed to stay
   on until they're 65 now, because the
   thing now seems to be that they're
   offering so many people a deal. I don't
   know what kind of a deal it is, mind,

but it must be quite acceptable before
they're taking it. Most of them are
retiring now at 62, or even 60.
(Worker, aged 57 years)

Table 3.1

Current workers: views on the prospect of
continuing with present job to 65 years

	No.	Per cent
Did not think it possible	2	11.8
No problems envisaged	3	17.7
Not sure, or a positive response qualified in terms of health or changes in the work situation	12	70.6
Totals	17	100.1

It is also interesting that only a minority were
optimistic; projecting from the fact they
experienced no real difficulty with their jobs.
Perhaps it is significant that two of the three had
only been in their current jobs for around 18
months, and the third had spent the previous 6
years in an ancillary function following a heart
attack. All of them had, at the time of interview,
relatively light jobs.

Most men were uncertain of their prospects, or
qualified their optimism by an assumption of no
change in work demands and/or health circumstances.

Well, the only thing is if they put three
men on to the machine, as they're trying
to do now ... That leaves three of us
now; so I'll have to do more work.
Maybe in the next month or two I'll be
saying, 'Well I can't do it.'
(Worker, aged 61 years)

That's the only thing that's in the back
of everybody's mind, I think. You see,
we work a lot of hours. We are required,
sometimes, to work a lot of overtime.

> If you are taking on the likes of a
> twelve hour day, something like that,
> and you're working hard for twelve
> hours and you're nearly sixty-two;
> it takes it out of you, obviously.
> You begin to think, 'Well, I hope
> the heck I can carry on.'
> (Worker, aged 61 years)

In all, 14 of the 17 men (82.4 per cent) were
cautious or pessimistic about prospects of working
to the state pensionable age. The two factors
operating, in their view, were health uncertainties, and the ever-present prospect of changed
working situations that would invalidate their
experience, or make them surplus to the mill's
requirements.

THE DECLINE IN WORK ABILITY

Specific health problems - from rheumatoid knee
joints to heart conditions - constituted major
problems for some men. However, in an occupational
environment that often involved lifting, standing
for long periods and the rigours of shift work, a
more general question of fitness arose.

Table 3.2

Current workers: reactions to the idea
that a man's work deteriorates with age

	No	Per cent
Unqualified agreement, or agreement qualified with reference to compensatory characteristics	14	82.4
Unqualified rejection, or rejection qualified with reference to compensatory characteristics	3	17.7
Totals	17	100.1

Most of these men thought that work ability did
deteriorate with age, although some did qualify
their responses with the mention of compensating

qualities such as experience and carefulness.
Generally, they were conscious of the fact that, in
relation to work demands, they were not 'the men
they once were'.

> I know when we were shifting some gear
> the other day, and it was gear that I
> could normally ... that I've seen me
> [gestures] ... You suddenly realise
> that you can't throw things about like
> you used to be able to.
> (Worker, aged 54 years)

> I find it on night shift; especially
> on night shift. Up till about 2 o'
> clock in the morning you feel you're
> going OK then, after that, you seen to
> slow down a bit ... after a certain
> time. The '2 to 10' and the '6 to 2'
> is not too bad, but the night shift I
> found it ... You feel that you could
> sit down for a while but you've just
> to keep going. You do slow down after
> a certain age.
> (Worker, aged 62 years)

> You slow up in an awful lot of things,
> not just physical ... you slow up up
> here [points to head] as well ... It
> comes to be an effort if you want to
> do a thing and try to keep up with
> the young ones, you've got to be
> alert all the time before you can keep
> up with them ... and that's just for
> a start. If you're not yourself -
> you're sluggish - you can drop a
> clanger, and things like that.
> (Worker, aged 60 years)

> A lad of 20 would pick it up quicker
> than I would. I would still pick it
> up and, actually, once I had picked
> it up I believe I would do it better ...
> I get the impression with the older
> chap, once he's got it, it sticks
> better ... although it takes longer
> to get there.
> (Worker, aged 55 years)

While older workers did not draw a distinction
between intrinsic and reactive ageing effects
(Ward, R., 1979), their perceptions of

deterioration were influenced by job demands. Work
at the mill, even in the ordinary course of events,
often entailed experiences that young men would find
physically taxing. Process innovation amplified the
reactive effects at two different levels. First,
where metal torpidity was associated with ageing,
doubts were cast on continued participation in a
changing workplace. Second, in the context of
demanning, age became a 'master' trait (1) and
other worker characteristics assumed more of an
auxiliary role. This is not to say that age
obscured all else in the way that workers regarded
themselves, or were regarded by others; but it
came to occupy an increasingly central position in
those evaluations.

Given the sort of work they did, and the changes
that occurred in the workplace, it might be assumed
that older workers would have seen themselves as
being in a different category from other mill
workers. To a large extent that proved to be the
case. While Table 3.3 does not show that an over-
whelming number of older workers categorised themselves as different from other workers; its significance must be judged in relation to parallel
data gathered on workers at the council's Building
and Works Department.

Table 3.3

Current workers: extent to which they
thought of themselves as being in a
different category to other workers

	No.	Per cent
Considered themselves to be in a different category	8	47.1
Did not consider themselves to be in a different category	7	41.2
Not sure	2	11.8
Totals	17	100.1

Where the job was 'getting on top' of the older
man in terms of a particular health problem, concern
about 'slowing up', or where the work situation
afforded unfavourable comparisons with younger men,

older employees had come to define themselves as
'men apart'. Where older men were 'on top of the
job' in terms of having good working relationships
with younger men, or where lighter work disguised
any deterioration in work ability, then they were
not inclined to think of themselves in this way.
Different circumstances fostered different self-
images but, for all, Stoneywood was becoming a place
where the chances of undisturbed employment to the
state pensionable age were decreasing.

CHANGING JOBS IN LATE WORKING LIFE

Older workers perceived their future job prospects
with some caution, and acknowledged performance
deterioration. In these circumstances, what could
older workers do to manipulate their current jobs,
or secure others, so reconciling decline with
demand in their last few years of work?

    Given their age and the esoteric nature of their
skills and experience, opportunities in the
external labour market could not be described as
good. Although the Aberdeen area's unemployment
rate (7.2 per cent in January 1984) was low by
national standards, men over the age of 50 years
were in a weak position especially if they sought
employment commensurate with their experience and
current pay expectations.

    With the mill's recruitment and retention char-
acteristics, few respondents had any direct
experience of difficulty in getting a job once past
the age of 50. There was, however, an awareness
that the external labour market was tough.

    What are your options?

    Outside the mill? Zero!
    (Worker, aged 54 years)

Anyway, few would have considered moving away from
the mill at their time of life. The mill was a
known work environment with good as well as
problematic features; pay levels were high in
comparison with what an older man could reasonably
expect to earn elsewhere and, most importantly,
there was an occupational pension scheme that
gained salience as years of service accrued.

For job changing in later life, the frame of reference was invariably the mill itself but, even there, the search for lighter work presented a dilemma. If an older man sought a lighter job, he had to accept the fact that there might be penalties. Grading, shift pay and his eventual occupational pension could be adversely affected. Men who undertook such a course of action usually had no alternative.

> When you look at my circumstances,
> there's very few jobs left in the
> mill ... as I say, there used to be
> a good few before ... where you
> don't touch machinery.... I might
> dislike my own job as it is - a
> bit monotonous and things like that -
> but I know very well there's nothing
> else for me. It's a low-paid job;
> it's a lot lower pay than even my
> son here now.
> (Worker, aged 57 years)

Job changing in late working life was, however, by no means uncommon as new machinery and reorganisation required much internal mobility. In cases where older men had been moved by the firm, pay and hence occupational pensions were given some protection.

As Table 3.4 shows, for a substantial proportion of older workers and retirees their later years at the mill were anything but a routine extension of the work they had previously done. Of the retired men, 58.5 per cent had changed jobs at least once and current workers, despite their incomplete work histories, were not significantly different. Most of this job changing in late working life was internal labour mobility although, with the retired men, three had actually gained mill employment after the age of 54 years. In terms of the overall demanning strategy operative in recent years, this paradox is hard to explain. However, these men had been taken on in the early 1970s when the plant-wide repercussions of process innovation were much less in evidence, and there were still peripheral posts to be filled.

Table 3.4

Retired and current workers: extent of job changing between 54 years and retirement or interview

	Retired men		Current workers		All men	
	No.	Per cent	No.	Per cent	No.	Per cent
Same job at 54 years as at retirement or interview	17	41.5	9	52.9	26	44.8
Changed jobs at least once in that period	24	58.5	8	47.1	32	55.2
Totals	41	100.0	17	100.0	58	100.0

$(X^2 = 0.27$, Yates' Correction applied, 1 deg. f., not significant at 0.05 level)

Whether job changing occurred as a result of 'late entry' or internal transfer, it had the effect of extending late working life; providing a few more years, or months, of employment than would have otherwise been the case. Employment or redeployment had allowed men who were industrially senescent, who had marginally impaired health or were surplus to requirements in their former posts, to continue in the worker role.

A limited range of reasons was put forward for the job changes in later life. Other than the three retirees who had been late entrants because they were redundant, or had personal conflict in their former employment, all job changing was occasioned by poor health, reorganisation and discretionary redeployment. As indicated in Table 3.5, poor health and reorganisation had been the dominant reasons for internal transfer among both current and retired workers. The third category - termed discretionary redeployment - refers to action on the part of foremen and managers where industrial senescence was recognised, or feared. This might have happened because it was regarded as a kindness to an individual, or because it was

beneficial to the management of departmental work-
loads.

> Well, it wasn't a big store I was in.
> It was the small store that had the
> bothy (*). You'd to sort out all the
> bolts and nuts and prepare ... tackles
> and things what they were wanting for
> the jobs ... One of the foremen
> offered it to me ... just said, 'How
> about the store?'
> (Retired employee)
> (*) Bothy is used here to describe
>   a small room adjoining a work
>   area where tea breaks are taken.

Table 3.5

Retired and current workers: reasons for last
or only job change in late working life

	Retired men		Current workers		All men	
	No.	Per cent	No.	Per cent	No.	Per cent
Out of work	2	8.3	0	0	2	6.3
Personal conflict	1	4.2	0	0	1	3.1
Poor health	9	37.5	2	25.0	11	34.4
Reorganisat-ion	8	33.3	6	75.0	14	43.8
Discretionary redeployment	4	16.7	0	0	4	12.5
Totals	24	100.0	8	100.0	32	100.1

The relatively autonomous trade and ancillary
functions in the mill provided all the cases of
discretionary redeployment. Quite probably it was
not restricted to these functions, but it seems
likely that, in these areas, opportunities for
informal redeployment were more abundant. Even
where health circumstances were the precipitating
reason for a job change, redeployment could be
accomplished with the minimum of formality. The
account below - classified as a health related job
change - provides a cameo of what might be, given

the current demanning pressures, a vanishing form of
late working life redeployment.

> Under the circumstances, I was very well
> looked after. I wasn't forced to do
> overtime at all. I was ... I can quite
> truthfully say ... they looked after men
> very well indeed. They gave me light
> work in the latter years, before my
> major operations. I had minor operations
> to my knees before that, and they really
> did me well. I've no complaints.

> With the offer of lighter work, what
> actually did you do?

> Bench work; I didn't have the heavy
> work, going out into the mill and
> doing heavy work. If I went into the
> mill, I was doing maintenance of steel
> caps and things like that which was
> really light work. It really was
> light work, and I appreciated it.

> How did you get put on to light work?

> It was purely and simply understanding on
> the part of engineering management;
> there were no negotiations. I didn't
> put in a formal application. They just
> realised that I wasn't fit to do it.
> I'd been there for, say thirteen years,
> and the last three years they really
> looked after me very well. I can say
> that.
> (Retired employee)

Poor health circumstances and reorganisation
together triggered just over 86 per cent of all job
changing within the mill. To what extent, though,
did job transfers alter the work situation of
older men? Changing jobs, for many, could have
merely substituted one set of difficulties for
another; thereby providing little respite from
uncertainties and arduous conditions, and only
temporarily extending employment prospects.

THE NATURE OF THE JOB CHANGES

In an attempt to understand the overall nature of
the changes, jobs at 54 years (2), and at retirement

or interview, were analysed in terms of physical effort requirements, work patterns, functional roles, pace and interactional context. For ease of presentation, what happened to retirees over the complete span of their late working lives is considered first. Contrast with current employees is provided later in this chapter.

(a) Physical effort

Current workers and retirees were asked to evaluate jobs at 54 years and, if different, their present or last jobs in terms of a five-point scale that ranged from 'always light' to 'always heavy'. There were dangers inherent in this type of evaluation exercise, and it might have been useful to triangulate such gradings with 'official' class-ifications of the kind that Pearson (1957) had been able to use. However, the aim was not to create correspondence with official gradings, but to record respondent perceptions of the physical effort routinely required in the job, or jobs.

Table 3.6

Retired men: comparison of physical effort required by jobs at retirement

	Job changers at retirement		Non-changers at retirement		All men at retire-ment	
	No.	Per cent	No.	Per cent	No.	Per cent
Light/mostly light work	20	83.3	7	41.2	27	65.9
Always/mostly heavy or mixed physical demands	4	16.7	10	58.8	14	34.2
Totals	24	100.0	17	100.0	41	100.1

(p = 0.0066, significant at 0.01 level)

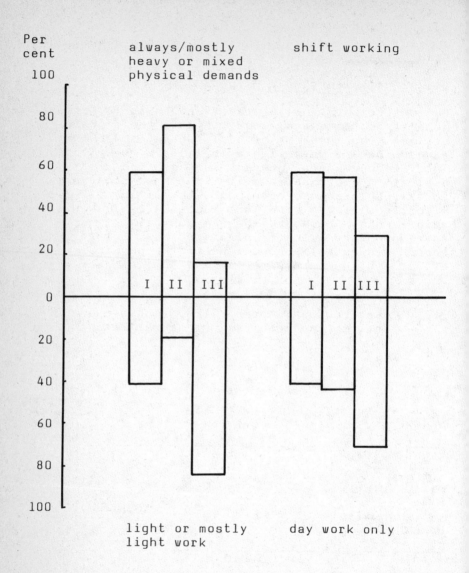

PHYSICAL EFFORT   WORK PATTERN

Per cent

always/mostly heavy or mixed physical demands

shift working

light or mostly light work

day work only

Figure 3.1   Retired men: comparison of jobs at 54 years and at retirement

FUNCTIONAL ROLE   JOB PACE   INTERACTIONAL
                                   CONTEXT

process   continuous   working with
                                   others

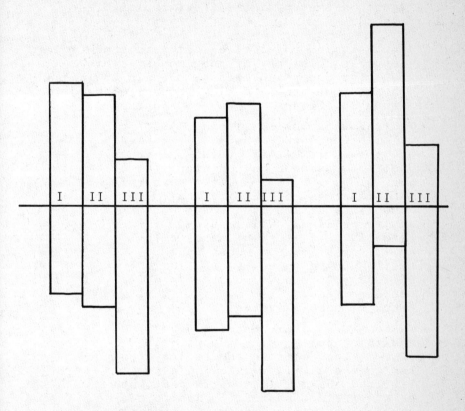

trade/ancillary   varied   working on
                                        own

KEY: I   - non-changers at 54 years, and at
               retirement
       II   - job changers at 54 years
      III   - job changers at retirement

For retired employees, as illustrated in Figure 3.1, jobs held at 54 years were most frequently described as heavy or mixed in their physical demands. In fact 71.1 per cent of all retired men rated their jobs at that age in these terms. While men who subsequently changed their jobs tended to be doing heavier work than those who did not change, the difference between the two groups was not statistically significant. However, at the point of retirement, changers and non-changers showed a wide divergence in the physical effort reported for their jobs.

A lightening of physical effort requirements was, in general, a corollary of job change. This was important for older men because even in the present mill environment, replete with mechanical handling equipment, some manual jobs were rigorous.

> You're not actually lifting, you're
> pulling the work. You've air tables,
> and things like that, to assist you ...
> [but] ... as soon as you stop, the
> work stops ... It's a purely physical
> job. There's some of it, what,
> roughly about 100 pounds weight that
> you're pulling. Well, say you
> actually cut 4 tons of paper on a
> shift, or 5 tons of paper on a
> shift, you're actually handling 10
> because you're pulling it off and
> shoving it on.
> (Worker, aged 57 years)

> We shifted a stack of calenders, the
> cheeks of which - the supporting
> sides - they were in the region of 6
> ton apiece ... They were 25 feet
> high and the ceiling was 29 feet, so
> we'd 4 feet of space in which to rig
> up lifting tackle to elevate these
> cheeks up to vertical.
> (Retired employee)

(b) Work pattern

Many of the mill's manual workers were employed on a shift basis. Paper production continued throughout the day and night with a few hours shutdown, for maintenance, on Saturdays. Shift work - mostly on a 6 a.m. to 2 p.m., 2 p.m. to 10 p.m. and 10 p.m.

to 6 a.m. basis - was an integral feature of better-
paid production jobs and was, therefore, accepted
or at least tolerated by men in that line of work.
Some men saw the shift system as a frame-work of
limitations on their life, while others prized the
flexibility offered by 'non-standard' free time
(3).

> I hated shift work ... I used to say that
> the man who invented shifts never worked
> them ... the most unsocial thing in the
> world. I will say with shift work that
> you've more time to yourself. If you're
> a golfer or something like that, it's
> ideal; but not being a golfer or
> angler, I couldn't stand them.
> (Retired employee)

> I prefer shifts to day ... I've got more
> time to myself, as it were ... Mind,
> I'm not so keen on this night shift as
> I used to be. I used to think nothing
> of it before; now it takes some thought
> to get up from the fireside at 9
> o'clock, you know.
> (Worker, aged 63 years)

Although some built their lives around shift work
patterns, and would have found day work a constraint, it was probably more the fact that production jobs, and pay differentials, were associated
with the shift system that dissuaded men from
seeking out the few day work opportunities that
existed. For men who worked on the making process,
such opportunities were rare and were associated
with a move to peripheral work.

> I worked shifts all my life, more or less.
> I never got the opportunity for day
> work ... there was one or two, prior to
> me going away [off sick], who got on to
> day shift, but they were only sort of
> going around painting and cleaning.
> (Retired employee)

> You've very little chance of getting a
> day shift job. It would be just
> scuttering about, you know, doing odd
> jobs here and an odd job there ...
> Then they'd want you to go back on
> shifts, somebody off sick, or somebody
> on holiday ... So, you're just as well

keeping in the shift anyway.
(Worker, aged 62 years)

Day working posed other problems as some jobs were
manned on a day-rota basis. Where this applied,
there was a perpetuation of some of the shift
system's disadvantages.

It changes every week. You get, maybe,
Tuesday or Friday, and the next week
you'll get Wednesday and Thursday; the
following week you'll get Friday and
Saturday and Sunday, and then Saturday
and you come back again. It rotates,
that's how it works, but you won't get
every weekend off.
(Worker, aged 61 years)

Table 3.7

Retired men: comparison of work
patterns at retirement

	Job changers at retirement		Non-changers at retirement		All men at retirement	
	No.	Per cent	No.	Per cent	No.	Per cent
Shift	7	29.2	9	52.9	16	39.0
Day only	17	70.8	8	47.1	25	61.0
Totals	24	100.0	17	100.0	41	100.0

(not significant at 0.05 level)

Although there were drawbacks to the relinquish-
ment of shifts, it was a consequence of some job
changes. For one or two men, it appeared as a major
factor in their late working life career.

Well, I was on shift work most of my
working life, but I had two major
operations and in the last stages I
asked for day shift ... so I got a
certificate from the doctor advising
it ... it was a wee bit of a struggle
to go onto day shifts. That was a
year before I retired, so I was more
or less breaking myself in. I was

home every night at five o'clock.
(Retired employee)

At 54 years, 42.1 per cent of all retirees had
been on day work, with subsequent job changers and
non-changers at 42.9 per cent and 41.2 per cent
respectively. Just before retirement, 70.8 per
cent of the job changers had day work although,
as Table 3.7 shows, the differences were not
statistically significant. Where older men gave up
shift work they also, to a large extent, gave up
process work and moved to ancillary tasks. At
retirement only 20 per cent of the process workers,
but 75 per cent of the ancillary personnel, worked
on a day-only basis.

(c) Functional role

In their mid-fifties, men who subsequently changed
jobs differed only slightly from non-changers in
their distribution over the three functional areas
of work. At 54 years, 58.8 per cent of non-
changers and 52.4 per cent of changers had been
engaged in some kind of process activity. In the
course of changing jobs, however, the latter group
changed their functional distribution quite noticeably, with a significant movement away from process
jobs.

Table 3.8

Retired men: comparison of functional
roles at retirement

	Job changers at retirement		Non- changers at retirement		All men at retirement	
	No.	Per cent	No.	Per cent	No.	Per cent
Process	5	20.8	10	58.8	15	36.6
Trade and ancillary	19	79.2	7	41.2	26	63.4
Totals	24	100.0	17	100.0	41	100.0

(p = 0.0153, significant at 0.025 level)

75

Traditionally, men who could no longer work in a
process capacity - by virtue of health, fitness or
role redundancy - were placed in peripheral activities as trade labourers, gatemen, storemen and so
forth.

His job was in the Sanatorium - the
Dispatch Department. They used to
speak about it being the Sanatorium ...
where all the old people, ill people
were.
(Retired employee speaking of his
brother)

The environment ... [in Dispatch] ...
is much better; the hours are more
stable, the work is more easily
defined and carried out - a lot of
mechanical handling aids etc ...
We have a number of machine men, ex-
machine men, who moved there after
several years in the machine room
where environments are, frankly,
very rigorous.
(Company manager)

As manning levels decreased with plant modernisation, older process workers ended up with jobs
that were auxiliary to the main productive activity
at the mill.

Well, quite honestly, the way I was
fixed in the mill ... every machine
I went near seemed to get made
redundant, you know. I was on the
pasting machine for years, that got
the chop. And then I went down to
the making department. I was on the
saturator; it got the chop. And
finally I landed up, the last three
years, in the printing department.
We had a wee guillotine there, and
you'd all the cutting, and fetching
and carrying and I really enjoyed
that job ... I see they've done away
with that now as well. The boys cut
their own labels, and stuff like that.
That was a lovely little job. I got
messages to do, and you met people.
You weren't stuck on the same machine
all the time, all day, you know. On
the pasting machine, I was there for

76

years and years ... At one time, once you
got on a machine, no matter what it did,
if you were any good at all they kept you
on there. I mean, I put in quite often
for foreman jobs, and things like this,
but they'd never ... I mean, that was
your job and that was it.
(Retired employee)

This account contained two points that were of
general significance. First, there was use of the
diminutive for the final job. It was referred to as
a 'lovely little job', and later in the interview he
similarly referred to the printing department work
as a 'nice wee jobbie'. Although the move was
favoured, in relation to age and the possible
alternatives, the linguistic style adopted perhaps
betrayed an awareness of job retrogression rather
than straight forward horizontal mobility. Second,
there was reference to the identification of man and
job in the mill. Movement between functional areas
underlined the fact that job changes in late working
life were something quite different from those
which may have occurred earlier in the worker's
life. It was a change in the type of work with
which a man had previously been identified.

(d) Job pace

For those directly involved in paper production,
pace was determined by the operating speed of
process machinery. For some, the 'continuous'
nature of their job meant continuous physical
effort; for others it meant continuous vigilance.
In fact, process innovation tended to change many
job demands, and while some work remained physically taxing throughout the shift, other jobs became
that much easier:

    ... instead of watching paper or, what I
    say, cutting up paper the right size,
    they're wanting you to stand and look
    down at it. You had to move a lot of
    wheels backwards and forwards, backwards
    and forwards, backwards and forwards,
    but now you've got what we call a 'magic
    eye' ... a camera. You can pick it up,
    and the figures come up on your machine,
    and you leave them. They usually run
    about the figures you want, they usually
    run between two sets of figures ... 10

77

to 15. Over that, you've to start shifting
about, you know. It's a lot simpler now ...
the job ... than it used to be. Instead
of standing for hour after hour, standing,
looking, putting back ... Now and again
you get a bad reel of paper, and you've
to go back to the old way again ...
standing, pushing ... but it's a lot
easier now.
(Worker, aged 62 years)

In consequence of a change in functional role, or
redeployment within the changing process function,
some men simultaneously managed to gain work that
was more varied in its demands. While it was the
case that even at 54 years, 55.2 per cent of all
jobs were described as varied; at retirement,
75.6 per cent had this kind of work.

Table 3.9

Retired men: comparison of job pace
at retirement

	Job changers at retirement		Non-changers at retirement		All men at retirement	
	No.	Per cent	No.	Per cent	No.	Per cent
Continuous	3	12.5	7	41.2	10	24.4
Varied	21	87.5	10	58.8	31	75.6
Totals	24	100.0	17	100.0	41	100.0

(not significant at 0.05 level)

From a similar base position in their mid-fifties
(58.8 per cent and 52.4 per cent of subsequent non-
changers and changers), 87.5 per cent of the latter
ended up with varied work demands. Given the
relatively high incidence of varied work at 54
years, in this sample, the differences between non-
changers and changers at retirement were not,
however, statistically significant.

(e) Interactional context

Many jobs in the process, trade or ancillary functions involved small-group working. With process
work, group size was fairly stable although there
were indications that teams were tending to become
smaller under the pressure of reduced labour
requirements from new machinery, and a general
slimming of the workforce.

> There's two of us on each machine, but
> they're trying to get three men on the
> two machines now, you see. They're
> cutting down again, so that's going to
> give us more work, you see.
> (Worker, aged 61 years)

Trade and ancillary functions sometimes required
group working but, particularly in the case of trade
jobs, group size varied according to the task in
hand.

> You definitely worked in a team ...
> various teams. You'd go out and
> take a stack of calenders, and that
> would possibly entail four or five
> men. Sometimes you'd just be doing
> pumps; you'd have yourself and a
> mate, but it was purely a matter of
> arrangement ... the nature of the job.
> (Retired employee)

> You're usually working with a team.
> I mean, sometimes you're working on your
> own; sometimes with one other person,
> and then sometimes you may be working
> with a bunch of six, you know. It all
> depends on what is wanting to be
> maintained.
> (Worker, aged 61 years)

Late working life job changing often involved a
change in the interactional context of work; a movement to solitary working conditions. At 54 years,
29.0 per cent of all retirees had worked on their
own, but this applied to 61.0 per cent at retirement. At 54 years, 14.3 per cent of the subsequent
job changers were working on their own but, for
non-changers, the figure was 47.1 per cent. Although these differences were not statistically significant, they might be construed as a factor in the
determination of late working life careers.

Working in groups at 54 years would have made an older man more liable to change jobs, because the work that called for these arrangements was the most arduous kind, or a likely target for technological change. At retirement, job changers had moved decisively away from even dyadic work contexts; 70.8 per cent were working on their own. However, as Table 3.10 indicates, the differences between changers and non-changers at the point of retirement were not statistically significant.

Table 3.10

Retired men: comparison of
interactional context at retirement

	Job changers at retirement		Non-changers at retirement		All men at retirement	
	No.	Per cent	No.	Per cent	No.	Per cent
Working on own	17	70.8	8	47.1	25	61.0
Working with at least one other man	7	29.2	9	52.9	16	39.0
Totals	24	100.0	17	100.0	41	100.0

(not significant at 0.05 level)

LATE WORKING LIFE CAREERS

When the jobs of the now-retired men were analysed in terms of the five work features, there were clearly discernible differences in the circumstances of those who continued in the job they had held in their mid-fifties, and those who changed. The jobs acquired by changers were varied but, typically, the work was lighter or less demanding than before. Figure 3.2 shows the kind of changes that could occur in the context of mill employment; at least in the experience of retirees.

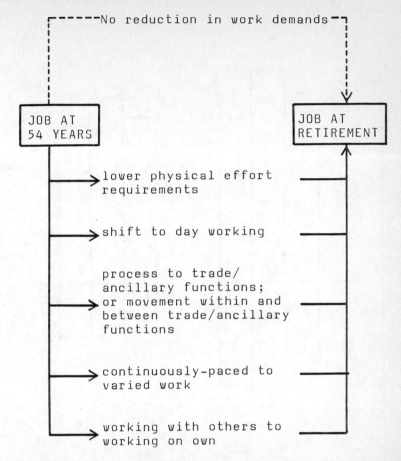

Figure 3.2 Light work acquisition in the mill

Retirees who changed jobs within the mill often managed to secure several of these light work features, and thereby substantially altered their work situation. As Table 3.11 shows, only 19 per cent changed jobs in a way that gave little or no respite from their former work circumstances, and 81 per cent gained at least two aspects of light work. In fact, 66.7 per cent had secured three or more.

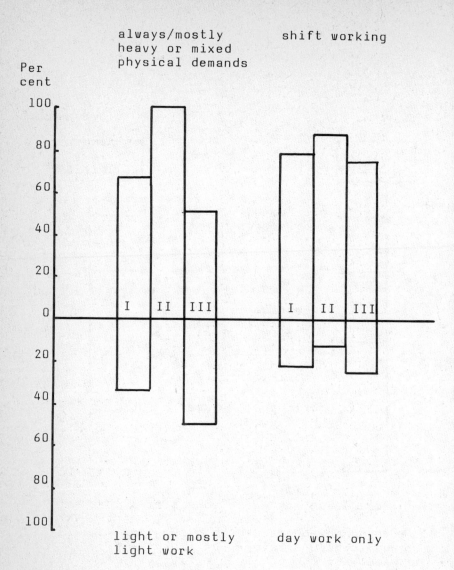

PHYSICAL EFFORT   WORK PATTERN

always/mostly   shift working
heavy or mixed
physical demands

Per
cent

light or mostly   day work only
light work

Figure 3.3   Current workers: comparison of
               jobs at 54 years and at
               interview

FUNCTIONAL ROLE   JOB PACE   INTERACTIONAL
                                       CONTEXT

  process   continuous   working with
                                       others

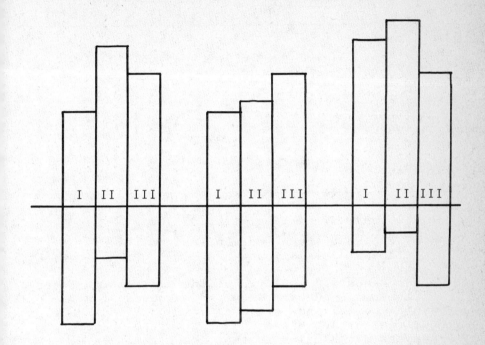

        I II III   I   II III   I   II III

trade/ancillary   varied   working on own

<u>KEY</u>:   I - non-changers at 54 years and at
                    interview
        II - job changers at 54 years
       III - job changers at interview

                          83

Table 3.11

Retired and current workers: aspects of light work gained in the last or only job change in late working life

	Retired men		Current workers		All internal job changers	
	No.	Per cent	No.	Per cent	No.	Per cent
Two or more aspects of light work gained	17	81.0	3	37.5	20	69.0
One or no aspects of light work gained, or reversal involved	4	19.0	5	62.5	9	31.0
Totals	(*)21	100.0	8	100.0	29	100.0

(p = 0.037, significant at 0.05 level)

(*) = excludes three men who entered the mill after the age of 54 years

Older men still employed at the mill showed, even with the small numbers involved, a somewhat different experience of late working life. While the extent of job changing among current older employees was similar to that among retirees, changes did not yield the same kind of results.

As illustrated in Fig. 3.3, job changing among current older employees produced only marginal alteration in their circumstances. There was, at best, a tendency to weakly reproduce the pattern of light work acquisition seen for retirees. At worst, as in relation to 'job pace', more job changers at interview were employed on work they described as continuous in its demands than had been the case at 54 years, or among non-changers.

With the small numbers involved, there is a danger of reading too much into data on job changes among currently employed older men. However, it is worth considering their circumstances even if conclusions have to be tentative.

Given that older workers had incomplete employment histories, it was possible that they would be involved in further changes which might result in jobs at retirement having similar characteristics to those that had been held by retirees. This would appear to be an unlikely scenario because the firm was facing a shortfall of light work posts; something that even some retirees had commented on.

> Well, there's quite a few, over the years,
> that I've seen not fit to cope with a
> certain job in the mill, and getting a
> day shift. But they're not so keen now
> to give you light duties as they used to
> be because there's not the jobs for
> them ... 'How long did it take to get a
> light job for me?' ... [to wife] ... It
> took months and months.
> (Retired employee)

> We've all got to put our houses in order
> in terms of productivity. What it's meant
> is that jobs ... have disappeared; gone.
> It's a case of one machinist and a new
> recruit, not three plus 'Fred Smith' who's
> on his way out. At the other end of the
> scale, of course, the young people are
> hit as well. We don't carry the spares,
> or the training spares, we used to ...
> should do. It's suicide to have anything
> other than the scheduled complement ...
> there are certainly not the opportunities
> for lighter, light type, jobs.
> (Company manager)

Redeployment occurred in the wake of process innovation and general reorganisation, but it appeared that the jobs gained were straightforward replacements rather than light work posts. This apparent change in the nature, if not the extent, of job changing arguably has important implications for the structure of late working life careers.

(a) The extension pattern

With this type of late working life career an employee entered retirement from the same job that

JOB CIRCUMSTANCES

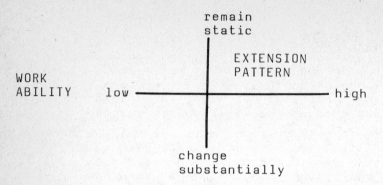

Figure 3.4   Optimum conditions for extension
pattern late working life career

he had held in his mid-fifties. Such a career
required that two conditions were satisfied. First,
that the job itself lasted for this period, i.e. the
position remained intact in spite of the extensive
changes that reduced the number of men necessary
to produce paper, and the general demanning that
limited numbers in trade and ancillary roles.
Second, role performance had to be maintained at a
satisfactory level. Health characteristics had to
remain stable, and the older man had to believe in
his ability to perform task requirements up to the
point of retirement.

For 41.5 per cent of the retirees, this combination of circumstance and orientation had existed,
although their late working lives tended to be
shorter than those of men who changed jobs in this
period. Job changers and non-changers differed
little in mean average age at retirement (63.8
years for changers and 62.4 years for non-changers),
but it was notable that of those who had continued
to work until they were 65 years, 70 per cent had
changed jobs in their last 11 years at the mill.
Only 30 per cent of those men who had retired at
the state pensionable age had extension career
patterns in their late working life.

(b) The transition pattern

Here, the job held at 54 years had not been the

same one as at the point of retirement. Moreover,
the job immediately prior to retirement tended to
have characteristics which clearly distinguished it
from previous jobs. Changes in functional role,
job pace, work pattern, interactional context, and
physical effort requirements coalesced in different
ways to give final jobs a lighter or less-demanding
character. Of the 41 retirees, 24 changed their
jobs in late working life; 21 (87.5 per cent) of
them within the mill. Of these internal job
changers, 81 per cent had secured at least two
aspects of light work and had, thereby, altered
their work situation in a substantial fashion.

    Internal job changers embarked on transitional
careers either because their jobs disappeared
amidst process innovation and reorganisation at the
mill, or their work ability deteriorated in terms
of objective health problems or industrial
senescence. As Figure 3.5 suggests, the optimum
conditions for transition pattern careers were where
low work ability, and substantial job change
combined. However, whether transitional careers
materialised even under these conditions was very
much dependent on the opportunities afforded by the
technical division of labour; and management
willingness to redeploy older men in this way.

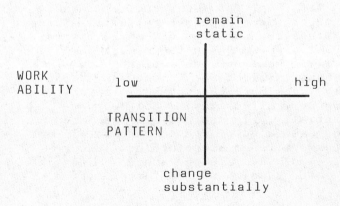

JOB CIRCUMSTANCES

remain
static

WORK
ABILITY   low   high

TRANSITION
PATTERN

change
substantially

Figure 3.5   Optimum conditions for transition
              pattern late working life career

DISCUSSION

At Stoneywood Mill it had been a tradition that
older workers were redeployed if they became
industrially senescent, or they suffered health
impairment. The complex technical division of
labour at the mill provided opportunities for this
kind of redeployment, and the long history of
paternalism shaped managerial attitudes to older
employees. A large measure of employment protection was afforded older men in this industrial
context. As the data on retirees has shown, many
older men were allowed to reach state pensionable
age at the mill via light work which offset the
effects of industrial senescence and, as far as
possible, health problems.

Process innovation and changed product markets
had, however, imposed strains on this traditional
employer/older employee relationship. Opportunities
for light work diminished at the same time as the
older worker's role became more marginal. What was
seen in the late working life of retirees was the
latter end of a long-standing pattern of older
worker redeployment, where industrial senescence
had been amplified by radical changes in the workplace; and where health difficulties could be less
easily accommodated.

Late working life had, for all these men, been
a period of change. Some remained in familiar jobs
while the workplace changed around them; others
found themselves in new jobs in their last few
years at the mill. Well over half of the now-
retired men became involved in job changes that
were, typically, much more than cosmetic alterations to known work situations. Their work
changed substantially. Though not all such men
experienced the same kind of change, or had all
prior job features altered, the internal labour
mobility of late working life had a near-uniform
direction; a retrogression of the former work
role.

Current workers looked set for a more limited
range of options as they moved further into their
late working lives. The opportunities necessary
for transitional careers were diminishing at a
time when one of the primary conditions for

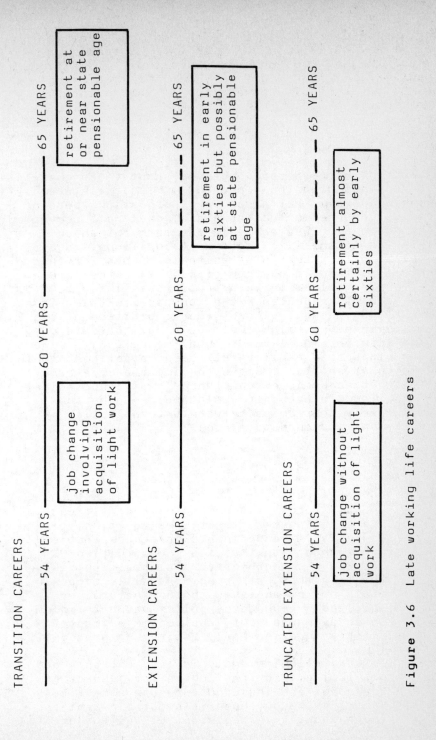

Figure 3.6   Late working life careers

89

extension career patterns - the integrity of existing jobs - was less likely to be realised. Those who had changed jobs since their mid-fifties had acquired light work only to a limited extent although, as indicated earlier in this chapter, comment on their situation has to be qualified by recognition of small numbers and the outside possibility of further job changes between interview and retirement.

Current workers were cautious about their chances of continuing in their present jobs to the state pensionable age, but these were perceptions born of radical change in the workplace, and the observation that demanning was age-related, rather than an illusion to the likelihood of transitional careers. Indeed, with a dearth of suitable niches for this career pattern to operate effectively, the future for current older workers would most likely take the form of truncated extension careers (see Figure 3.6). Job change, without the acquisition of light work dimensions, might well be a common feature of such late working lives though the period, allied to more widespread earlier retirement practices, would tend to be shorter. Given the impasse created by difficult economic circumstances and technological change, such a scenario would appear to be the most likely compromise between paternalistic management and industrial reality.

NOTES

(1)   Hughes (1945, p. 355), in his examination of social status, did not specifically focus on age as a 'master' trait; using it only in an 'auxiliary' sense in his reference to the 'boy wonder' epithet for incongruities between age and hierarchical position. Given the fact that, at Stoneywood Mill, demanning could not be achieved through natural wastage, and a redundancy policy was not implemented by management, age became a 'master' trait triggering early retirement possibilities.

(2)   In the following analysis late entrants are not included in the figures for jobs at 54 years but are included for jobs at retirement. Although there is a certain arbitrariness about this decision, it was thought to

90

provide a better reflection of the realities
of job changing at the mill given that the
three late entrants changed <u>occupations</u> as
well as <u>employers</u>. Their job changes could
not be effectively analysed in terms of the
five work features used with internal job
changers.

(3)   The issue of feelings towards shiftwork was
not systematically explored in the present
study. Wedderburn's (1980) analysis suggests
a complex relationship between worker
circumstances and attitudes. The proportion
of older workers in Wedderburn's study was
not, however, very great and their apparent
satisfaction with shifts might arguably be
associated with their recognition of a
weak labour market position.

4 The Building and Works Department

At Stoneywood Mill, the work and market situation of older men had been altered because the market for paper products became more competitive, and the new manufacturing machinery adopted in response to these changed conditions had lower labour requirements. The 'indulgency pattern' (1) which had developed with industrial paternalism came under threat, but continued to find expression in managerial efforts that facilitated transition careers. There were some indications from the data that, in terms of both management thinking and worker expectations, this strategy would have a more limited application in the future as opportunities for light work diminished. Early retirements were likely to become the main thrust of personnel policy for handling older workers' reduced utility.

   At the Building and Works Department, there were also pressures on older workers and management. There were, however, important differences between the two organisations. First, the department's capacity to facilitate transition careers was severely limited; there being a relative scarcity of light work posts realistically available for internal transfers. However, the repair and maintenance work of the department was, arguably, light work in relation to that which would commonly be found in the private sector. To this extent, it could be regarded as an enclave within the local labour market for building trades workers and, typically, it was most attractive to middle-aged and older men who put a higher value on steady employment than wage levels. Second, managerial willingness to subsequently redeploy older workers in the event of some health impairment, or industrial senescence, was constrained by a sequence of political pressures. Any 'sheltering' of older employees was discouraged as, directly and indirectly, legislation fostered the idea of competitiveness with the private sector. Here, too, was a changing context for late working life.

A CREATURE OF STATUTE

Although the department, per se, had been in existence for less than a decade when the research started, public works involving directly employed labour had long been a feature of Aberdeen. In one sense, then, the organisation had a fairly substantial local history, but it would seem appropriate to focus on legislative changes that had shaped its present structure and style of operations. The historical dimension in what follows is, therefore, short compared with the treatment of Stoneywood Mill, but legislation had the effect of creating major organisational discontinuities and it was the revamped conditions that dominated late working lives.

(a) Regionalisation

Under cumulative legislation dating back to 1889, Aberdeen had the status of 'County of City' which carried powers and responsibilities broadly equivalent to those of county boroughs in England and Wales. With this remit, the Corporation of the City of Aberdeen operated a public works (2) labour force as part of the City Engineer's Department. By the early 1970s, a broad spectrum of work was undertaken by this directly employed labour encompassing work in relation to roads, water supply and sewerage systems as well as repair and maintenance for schools, public buildings and the housing stock of the Corporation.

The 'County of City' status was, however, subject

to the pressures of local government reform. The
Scottish Office White Paper (The Modernisation of
Local Government in Scotland, 1963), the Wheatley
Report (Royal Commission on Local Government in
Scotland, 1969), and the government White Paper
(Reform of Local Government in Scotland, 1971) all
acknowledged the need for radical reform, and
served to shape central government policy which
found definitive expression in the Local Government
(Scotland) Act of 1973. Although there was
variance in both emphasis and detail (Alexander,
1982) between these policy precursors and the
eventual Act, one feature remained constant - the
stated belief that the system of local government
in Scotland had become unwieldy and a reallocation
of responsibilities should take place.

Public works operations of the old City Corporation were, from the May 1975 implementation date of
the 1973 Act, split between the new upper tier of
local government - Grampian Region - and the new
lower tier - Aberdeen District Council. Grampian
Region became the relevant authority for education,
roads, sewerage and water leaving a much reduced
range of functions for public works personnel with
the new Aberdeen District Council. They were left
with maintenance, repair and environmental work for
the housing schemes and council buildings with some
agency work for other authorities. Certain
categories of work were, therefore, transferred to
regional level along with a substantial number of
men and, as outlined in Chapter 5, some of the
transferred work had been important for employees
when the weather was too bad for outside work.
Some men even regarded the 'lost' work as the
most interesting kind.

> When regionalisation came in there was
> a big difference. A great deal of work
> was taken from us then ... The more
> interesting work was taken from us -
> schools, clinics, that sort of thing -
> lost all that ... a considerable amount
> of work. It was surprising how we
> were able to carry on.
> (Retired employee)

Along with the much-heralded changes to local government areas and responsbilities, there was, in the
preceding policy development period, a related
concern with the management structure for the new

system. The terms of reference for the Wheatley
Report (Royal Commission on Local Government in
Scotland, 1969) did not require recommendations on
the internal organisation of the new local authorities, but it did consider the issue. However, as
Rhodes and Midwinter (1980) argue, it provided only
limited insights on the detail of management. How
the administration of the new responsibilities was
to be organised was the subject of a separate
investigation which resulted in the Paterson Report
(The New Scottish Local Authorities; Organisation
and Management Structures, 1973).

The combined effects of the 1973 Act and the
Paterson Report meant a radical change for public
works operations in Aberdeen. Large district
councils, such as Aberdeen, where there would still
be substantial public works activity, were
recommended to form separate direct works departments headed by a manager of 'Director' level. In
May 1975, then, not only were functions changed in
accordance with the 1973 Act, but surviving
functions were to be handled by a newly constituted
and separate department - Aberdeen District Council
Building and Works Department.

(b) Restructuring

Along with functional changes came a relocation of
public works operations to a purpose-built office
and depot complex in Kittybrewster, Aberdeen. The
move from Jasmine Terrace, which had been occupied
by public works personnel since 1897, was more than
a re-siting of the central depot, however, it was a
component in a broader scheme of organisational
change - decentralisation.

There were two elements in this organisational
change. First, it involved a decentralisation of
operations. Manual workers most regularly engaged
in repair and maintenance on the housing schemes
were dispersed to bases in these areas. Depots at
Mastrick, Northfield, Hilton, Seaton, Torry and
Kincorth were already in existence, but were
primarily used for materials storage, and as a base
for workers. These depots were up-graded to become
operational sub-units of the department, with the
result that relatively few building trades workers
were left at the central depot in Kittybrewster.
This plan was promoted in the name of operational

efficiency (Minutes of the City of Aberdeen
District Council 1977-1980, pp. 2264 - 2265), a
theme that was to gather momentum in the next few
years. The second dimension of decentralisation
was administrative restructuring, a change that
overshadowed operational and personnel relocation.
Supervision was to pass from trade foremen, who
had traditionally been the administrative front
line, to multi-trade supervisors in each of the
reconstituted depots. The idea was not to create
an additional layer of authority under the super-
intendents, who had broad territorial responsibilities, but to replace foremen altogether in the main
trades.

The authority structure had previously contained
foremen, sub-foremen and chargehands for each
trade. Only the latter grade men were 'on the
tools'; foremen and sub-foremen were administrative personnel although the post-regionalisation
development of the department, with growth in the
number of white collar employees, had caused some
atrophy of their role.

> I was responsible only to the manager
> and the deputy-manager. There was a
> foreman to every section, you see ...
> plumbing, building, you know. We
> controlled our own men, we hired and
> fired; and bought materials ...
> and did the whole bit, you know.
> But it gradually changed. The office
> staff was increased. Estimators
> came in ... you see we used to do
> estimating as well ... Buyers came
> in ... co-ordinators, all sorts of
> people came in finally. Our duties
> became less and less, 'admin-wise'.
> It gave us more time to go out and
> supervise, but it wasn't quite so
> interesting for me.
> (Retired employee)

The concept of multi-trade supervision obviously
presented problems to existing trade foremen and
sub-foremen. In the first place, it cut across
the conventional authority system causing doubts
about the effectiveness of the new proposals and,
for some, doubts about their ability to undertake
this wider span of control.

I was not prepared to carry out this job.
I thought it was ... well, we felt, and
I think we were right ... that the
electrical department should be run by
electricians ... I just felt that I was
better off getting out, because I
would never have been happy with the
job I was offered. I was going to be
in charge of plumbers, joiners,
painters ... which was divorced from
my trade. If I was to be asked any
technicalities about their trade, I
wouldn't be able to answer them.
That was the simple reason.
(Retired employee)

Secondly, the new structure allowed for fewer first-
line administrative personnel than had previously
been the case. Failure to get one of the new jobs
presented the choice of early retirement or
demotion.

You see, what happened was ... it was
up to anyone to apply for these
superintendent jobs, and supervisor's
jobs, which I was more or less qualified for ... I applied for the superintendent job. Never even got an
interview. So I got back saying that
I'd applied and that ... 'Sorry, the
job was filled' ... all official
writing, you know. Then I applied
for a supervisor's job, which was
only what I was doing then, more or
less, and again, no interview ...
They did away with foremen altogether.
Under the foremen was chargehands.
Well, I'd been a chargehand for
twenty one years before I was made
foreman, and it meant ... you see,
the chargehand's job is working with
tools and looking after men at the same
time ... but I didn't even get chance
of that and yet I'd been a chargehand
for twenty one years before that ...
Well, you see, if I'd stayed on there
as a joiner it would have meant that
I'd got a joiner's rate of wages;
paying superannuation at a joiner's

97

> rate so when I did become sixty-five
> I'd have only got a joiner's rate,
> you know. Whereas, at the moment,
> when I retired I got the foreman's
> rate for pension. So I'd really
> have lost money although I'd have
> still been working there ... I'd
> have lost money.
> (Retired employee)

Whatever the potential benefits of operational decentralisation, administrative restructuring caused direct problems for men who, because of the nature of promotion in these trades, tended to be in their late working life. The effects were not, however, limited to such men as ordinary tradesmen tended to resent this break from tradition.

> We had a foreman in charge of
> the mason's department, but
> nowadays it can be say, a joiner.
> He would be 'number one' up
> there, and he's in charge of
> different departments with the
> result that ... Well, you can
> look at the job, if you're in
> that trade, and say, 'Oh well,
> he'll need maybe sand, cement,
> bricks or stones, and this and
> that.' Whereas, a painter or
> a joiner would be looking at
> it and wouldn't have a bloody
> clue.
> (Worker, aged 56 years)

The new system went into operation in 1981 reinforcing, at departmental level, the goal of managerial efficiency which formally underwrote the central government enquiries of the 1960s, and provided justification for local government reorganisation in 1975. Even at departmental level, though, the quest was not limited to decentralisation and administrative restructuring.

(c) Work study and incentive bonus scheme

As far back as November 1966, the former Aberdeen City Council approved the use of a firm of management consultants to investigate the possibility of work study based incentive schemes in the City

Engineer's Department. The consultants' report
issued in April 1967 presented a scheme that was
subsequently adopted by the City Council.

This scheme survived local government reorganisation so, for the Building and Works Department as
it was named after 1975, the same basic incentive
bonus scheme was used as had applied to the public
works personnel in the 'old' City Engineer's
Department. Responsibility for the scheme's
operation, however, passed from the City Engineer
to the Director of Building and Works until
November 1976, when the function was transferred
to the Director of Manpower Services.

The application of work study to trades engaged
in diverse repair and maintenance activities was
not without its problems. The distinction made
by Dzierzek (1969) between the physical permanence
of the work place and the predictable cycle of
work in manufacturing industry, and the large
variations in site conditions and task difficulty
in the construction industry are very relevant.
In fact, it might be argued that repair and maintenance work, with all its inconsistency, makes the
application of work study even more questionable.
For manual employees and management alike, the
work study based incentive scheme caused problems.

First, 'standard values' were applied to the
vast majority of jobs, but there were 'grey areas'
in repair and maintenance work where dry-rot and
water penetration,for example, caused more
complexity than could be initially estimated.
Further, unusual trade circumstances such as the
use of special materials or techniques called for
'special' rather than 'normal' times to be
applied.

Second,as pay was directly linked to the
worker's ability to progress work within given
times, there was a danger that quality would be
subordinated to speed. Although this problem was
recognised, the incentive element was regarded as
crucial by officials involved with work study.
Quality control was essentially a supervisory
problem.

> Well, obviously, we say here that the times
> that have been arrived at are average
> times ... and we would expect that the
> man is motivated; and remember it is a
> so-called incentive scheme. I think
> sometimes people forget and, over the
> years, this has decayed and people
> expect the extra payment as merely part -
> as a right - of a basic rate of pay.
> (Official, Manpower Services Department)

With a 'standard performance' (3) of 100 BSI there
was frequent under and over performance varying
with individual workers, and the types of job they
had been engaged in during the week. There was an
element of flexibility in the managerial view of
actual performance, but when performance levels
were below 85 BSI or above 115 BSI, enquiries were
made.

Third, clerical effort was high throughout the
system - for manual workers and for white collar
staff.

> There are ten work study personnel of
> various grades involved in the routine
> processing of daily job sheets produced
> by Building and Works activities. The
> clerical demands are heavy with, for
> example, painterwork job sheet evaluation
> accounting for 80 per cent of one work
> study assistant's time, and general
> response joinery job sheet evaluation
> accounting for half the workload of
> another.
> (Official, Manpower Services Department)

For some manual workers, the quantification of time
for the actual task, cleaning up and travel
between the depot and the job, had brought an
unwelcome element to their jobs. Some men were
better than others at coping with the paperwork.

> This is another problem of the older men.
> They don't like writing, and there are
> certain cases, I think, where the man has
> not written in everything he has under-
> taken. The sharp pencil! If you're
> good at writing, that's fine. If you're
> not, you may leave something out so that
> when one of our lads comes round and
> says, 'What about the skirting board?'

And he says, 'I did that.' Well, it's
not on the sheet.
(Official, Manpower Services Department)

Fourth, the bonus earned varied between trade
groups. Although wages were, in all cases, calcul-
ated from three basic elements - the nationally
agreed basic rate, the bonus derived from a
'bonus calculator' figure, and overtime rates - the
first two elements did not have a consistent
relationship across all trades. Anomalies in the
amount of bonus earned caused a sense of grievance
for some when the precise mechanics of the last
national wage agreement became hazy.

Well, it's complex due to the national
negotiations. The national negotiators
play the ball game. The electricians,
over the last two years, played all
their rises on the basic rate of pay
with the result that their 'bonus
calculator' has dropped ... it's some-
where in the region of £99, but their
bonus calculator is only £51. So, if
you take a third of £51, it's about
£17 ... So, obviously, there's now a
moan in the system saying 'How does a
semi-skilled man get more than me on
bonus, when I am the skilled man?'
(Official, Manpower Services Department)

It wasn't really a very good bonus. It
started off ... it first started off
and you were guaranteed ... you got a
percentage of your wages anyway. But
as the years went on and your wages went
up, this differential never moved your
bonus. They never put the bonus up.
When I left there my earnings were
roughly about, say, £128 a week, but
your bonus was only earned on £55
instead of the whole rate which
it was when it first started off. There
was a bit of trouble with the bonus right
enough.
(Retired employee)

In spite of the difficulties associated with work
study and the incentive bonus scheme, further
tightening was imminent.

Because of the worsening political climate
for DLO operations, we are going to ask
men to work harder, faster, and usually
for less money with the main vehicle for
these changes to the working regime being
tighter control of the bonus scheme.
(Gallagher, 1984)

Two recent developments are likely to have
considerable impact on bonus schemes. It
has been fairly widely recognised that
some schemes were open to abuse and man-
ipulation, and one or two cases had received
a good deal of publicity. In some measure
as a result of this adverse comment and
partly because officers have been becoming
more concerned with obtaining value for
money from bonus schemes, perhaps through
the increasingly vigilant attitude of rate-
payers and auditors, it was agreed in 1980
by the Joint Negotiating Committee for
Local Authorities Services (Building and
Civil Engineering) (known as the JNC) that
all bonus schemes had to be reviewed by
their local authority and certified by
the JNC before the newly agreed bonus
calculator was to be applied.
(Department of the Environment/Audit
Inspectorate, 1983, p. 141)

   Revisions to the scheme used by Aberdeen District
Council were being considered with, on the one
hand, central government insistence that revised
schemes were speedily implemented and, on the
other, pleas for time and additional staff to
effect the changeover from the Director of Manpower
Services (Minutes of the City of Aberdeen District
Council, 17 October 1983).

   The detailed measurement of tasks, and the
relationship between performance and pay, were
features of the organisational environment which
added stress to late working life. Feelings about
'bonus' and 'work study' (see Chapter 5) were
influenced by individual experiences, but there was
every reason to suppose that a further tightening
of the system would be unwelcome to older men.

(d)   Competitiveness

While DLOs have a long history, they have had something of a Cinderella quality (4) with little
recognition of their role by elected representatives, or the public. Errors and costs were,
however, consistently noted by the private building
contractors' organisation - the National Federation
of Building Trades Employers - which accused local
authorities of 'feather-bedding' their workers, and
concealing the true cost of directly-employed
labour (Tilley, 1976).

During the latter half of the 1970s, attention
began to focus on the costs and benefits of DLOs
with a major role being played by the Chartered
Institute of Public Finance and Accountancy
(CIPFA) who argued that the accounts of DLOs
should be able to demonstrate cost effectiveness in
comparison with private sector alternatives (Flynn
and Walsh, 1982). Economic and political changes
in the late 1970s gave fresh impetus to this idea
as local government came under close scrutiny (5).

Within its first year of office, the new
conservative government issued a consultation
paper on DLOs (Department of the Environment,
1979), and incorporated specific proposals in the
Local Government Planning and Land Bill which
survived a stormy passage through Parliament
(Jacobs, 1980) to become the Local Government
Planning and Land Act 1980.

Part III of the Act (6) focussed specifically on
DLOs and contained statutory requirements that
radically altered the conditions under which they
were to operate. To prevent cross-subsidization,
work was divided into separate accounting categories (7), and in order to demonstrate the
financial efficiency of DLOs, it was required that
a 'rate of return' was made on the capital
employed (8). To further show that the authority
was making the best use of resources by directly
employing labour, the DLO had to compete for a
certain percentage of its work (9).

The Act, and the detailed performance directives
which came in its wake, caused a variety of
difficulties for DLOs (10). Flynn, Walsh and
Halford (1983) reported that while most agencies

managed to achieve the 5 per cent return on capital
employed in the first years (1981-2) of the Act's
operation in England and Wales, the results were
largely an illusion. The figures, they argue, were
a product of 'estimating and accountancy practices'
rather than 'operational efficiency', because
indication of the proportion of work won on tender
was not required for the first year's report.
Further, information received by the Institute of
Local Government Studies was said to reveal that
little work was gained in that way. If this was the
case, then the full impact of the legislation has
still to be seen, for new regulations (11) require
that 60 per cent of small maintenance jobs should
be put out for tender.

In Aberdeen, the problems were little different to
those reported for England and Wales, although a 26
per cent rate of return on capital employed was
reported for the first year of operation (1982-3)
under the new Act in Scotland (City of Aberdeen
District Council, September 1983). The first report
required by the Act started with the comment:

> The past year had undoubtedly been the
> most difficult in the existence of the
> Department of Building and Works.
> Concurrent with major changes in
> organisation, working arrangements and
> serious difficulties encountered with
> the newly introduced computerised
> costing and financial systems, the
> Department has had to contend with
> meeting the requirements of the Local
> Government Planning and Land Act 1980
> (Part III), effective in Scotland
> from 1st April 1982.
> (City of Aberdeen District Council,
> September 1983, p. 1)

The accountancy problems were more starkly revealed
in a local press report (Evening Express, 27 July
1983) in which the Director of Building and Works
stated that difficulties with the accounting system
meant that they had not been able to prepare
financial reports for the current period; they had
not completed their billing for last year, or
started this year's, and clients were receiving
bills with a proviso that they might have to be
adjusted once the financial position was
established. Further, the Director revealed that

solving the accountancy problems with the new system had 'diverted staff and resources from improving response maintenance' (Minutes of the City of Aberdeen District Council, 17 October 1983, p. 1061).

Table 4.1

Summary of major changes affecting manual workers in the Building and Works Department

	Implement- ation date	Effects on manual employees
Work study/ incentive bonus scheme	1967	formal emphasis on working efficiency that survives regi- onalisation in 1975
Local Government (Scotland) Act 1973	1975	some categories of work and about 200 men transferred to Grampian Region
Decentralisation and administrative restructuring	1981	changes to super- visory structure directly affect foremen and sub- foremen
		changes viewed with some cynicism by men used to the traditional authority structure
Local Government Planning and Land Act 1980	1982	increased stress on financial and operational efficiency
		target revisions increase depart- ment's difficulties

Later reports by the Building and Works Department (City of Aberdeen District Council, August 1984; City of Aberdeen District Council, September 1985) confirm Flynn, Walsh and Halford's depiction of ever-tightening financial circumstances. The rate of return on capital employed had fallen to 22 per cent for 1983-4, and to 8 per cent for 1984-5 with text comment on the inappropriateness of this measure of operational efficiency.

While the problems of financial management might appear esoteric they were an important component in the general tightening of circumstances for the department. The 1980 Local Government Planning and Land Act, and the financial directives which followed, added greater stress to the idea of operational efficiency with their iconic reference to private sector competitiveness. As Table 4.1 shows, the 1980 Act was a single, though extremely important, factor in changing the organisational circumstances of manual employees.

EMPLOYMENT AT THE BUILDING AND WORKS DEPARTMENT

(a) Overall levels of employment

With local authority activities being held in sharp focus by central government, particularly since 1979, there had been pressure on overall employment levels (12). Walsh (1983) has argued that while the labour-intensive nature of local government services made employment levels particularly vulnerable, the overall effect of central government restrictions had not been as pronounced on employment as on expenditure. Similarly, Travers (1983) in his analysis of Joint Manpower Watch statistics for England and Wales, suggests only a 'mild but widespread demanning' with considerable variation between different service sectors. Both accounts agree, however, that manpower cuts have fallen heaviest on manual workers, especially those in construction.

Prior to the 1975 implementation of the Local Government (Scotland) Act 1973, Aberdeen's public works personnel numbered 728 (Press and Journal, 23 December 1975) but with the resultant loss of functions - primarily roads and sewerage work - about 200 were transferred to the higher tier of

local administration, Grampian Region. The new
Building and Works Department concentrated its
efforts on housing maintenance and repairs, and
continued to operate in this way, although in the
early years of its existence there was some
discussion about development into new construction
work (Press and Journal, 23 December 1975; Press
and Journal, 16 November 1976; Evening Express,
16 November 1977). The limitation of functions, by
legislation and by District Council decision, meant
that the number of manual workers dropped from 503
in September 1976 to 384 in February 1980.
However, seasonal variations overlay the trend and,
in the last few years, there had been an increase
in employment bringing manual worker numbers to
around 430 by March 1983.

There was a strong argument that, in relation to
the demands placed on the department, manual worker
employment levels had to hold at this sort of level
if there was to be no reduction in service to
tenants.

> Now I don't know what the breakdown is
> of different trades, but I understand
> there's something like 100,000 (*) job
> tickets' turnover a year. So, you can
> see it's quite a heavy workload ...
> That demand will not go away particularly
> if you've got ageing housing stock.
> You're going to have more and more
> problems.
> (Official, Building and Works Department)
> (*) see footnote 13

In spite of this argument, it is difficult to be
sure about future levels of employment because,
first, the operation of the 1980 Act in Scotland is
one year behind England and Wales, and the most
recent tendering directives have yet to make their
impact. Second, continued financial stringency by
central government suggests that manual workers
will continue to bear the brunt of whatever manpower
cuts occur (Travers, 1982). It is, however, the
1980 Act which presents the most immediate threat
to employment in the department.

There is a general problem with the idea of DLO
competitiveness (ADLO News, September 1982; ADLO
News November 1983; Secker, 1983) with legal
restrictions on their ability to act as if they

were private sector firms. They can, for example, compete only for local authority or recognised agency work in a given territory; and they are unable to cross-subsidize in their tendering strategy because each work category must secure the specified rate of return. Additionally, as part of their service orientation, DLOs have to operate with difficulties that few private firms could handle. In a local press report highlighting the fact that emergency callouts cost almost £100,000 during the year, the Director of Building and Works was quoted as saying:

> ... while accepting that the credibility
> of DLOs depends to a considerable extent
> on competition as the only means of
> demonstrating that the authority obtains
> genuine value for money, the present
> high overheads added to a 5 per cent
> return on capital employed would, in
> my opinion, make it unlikely that an
> adequate amount of contract work could
> be gained in open competition.
> (Evening Express, 21 October 1981)

Adding weight to that claim, it was reported in 1983 that some £16,000 a year was added to costs simply by tradesmen being unable to gain access to premises (Press and Journal, 28 July 1983).

Attempts to achieve the precarious competitiveness required by the 1980 Act are likely to directly affect manpower strategies. Although overall employment levels at the Building and Works Department were being held, ever-increasing competition could alter the situation quite rapidly. General, or sectional, demanning is a spectre that has been recognised elsewhere.

> For example, if the authority cannot make
> the rate of return, this may be the
> result of the difficulties of one group
> of workers rather than the whole DLO.
> There may then be implicit or explicit
> pressure to get rid of that particular
> group. Painters have found themselves
> in particular difficulty in competing.
> (Flynn and Walsh, 1982, p. 54)

The application of this kind of thinking to the situation in Aberdeen is, unfortunately, more than a remote possibility. The Personnel and Management

Services Committee of Aberdeen District Council was,
towards the end of 1985, considering a report on
staffing from the Director of Building and Works.
In a session from which the press and members of
the public were excluded, redundancies and
retraining/redeployment were the options being
considered, and painters were the only trade group
mentioned in minutes that were otherwise devoid of
detail. At that meeting, the vote was for a
declaration of redundancies (Minutes of the City of
Aberdeen District Council, 2 December 1985).

   It would be wrong to infer overmuch from the
scant detail currently available, but it is also
hard to ignore the possibility that this is part of
the grim scenario intimated by Flynn.

> The new profit criteria will mean that
> the authorities will not be able to
> cushion the impact of the cuts on the
> labour force. Large scale redundancies
> are inevitable. The combination of the
> Act and the cuts in spending will
> destroy the one haven of stability in
> the otherwise unstable and uncertain
> construction industry.
> (Flynn, 1981, p. 59)

(b)   Career profiles and the local labour market

The Building and Works Department employees and
retirees who were interviewed had careers that
rested on occupation rather than a specific employing organisation. Local authority employment was,
typically, a feature of middle age when men ceased
trading their skills to the highest bidder in the
private sector building industry. None of these
men had started their working lives with the
council; and very few had joined in their
twenties.

   Private sector building firms offered little by
way of stable employment, laying men off in
recession and in bad weather, closing down when a
proprietor died, or going bankrupt. Some men had
spent their earlier years on short-term contracts,
working for a variety of local firms or chancing
their arm at self-employment.

Table 4.2

Building and Works Department sample: age on entry to the department or its City of Aberdeen Corporation predecessor

	Retired men		Current workers		All men	
	No.	Per cent	No.	Per cent	No.	Per cent
14-20 years	0	0	0	0	0	0
21-30 years	5	13.9	1	6.3	6	11.5
31-40 years	15	41.7	8	50.0	23	44.2
41-50 years	9	25.0	5	31.3	14	26.9
51-60 years	5	13.9	2	12.5	7	13.5
61 + years	2	5.6	0	0	2	3.9
Totals	36	100.1	16	100.1	52	100.0

Notes (a) Retired employees:

actual range 24 - 63 years
mean average 41.2 years

Current employees:

actual range 27 - 59 years
mean average 40.6 years

(b) Some men had worked for the council on
more than one occasion. Figures above
relate to their last, or current,
period of employment.

I got fed up of travelling and I came
back ... I was in Motherwell. These
people that I live with now, they were
the first people that I knew here
years ago - of course there's only two
of them left now - and I said, 'Bugger
this travelling. I'm fed up with
travelling, could I stop here?' And
they said, 'You can stop here as long
as you like.' So I stopped here and I
went down to the dole, and they said

this, that and the other ... not many jobs
at that time ... slack, you know. I said,
'Give me a green card, and let me go round
and get my own job if I can get one.' He
gave me a green card, and I came up the
top of Upper Mastrick Drive here ... the
Town was working there; they'd just
started to build Mastrick. I walks into
the office and there was (x); he was
the Town's gaffer at the time ... He says,
'What do you want?' I said, 'I'm looking
for a job.' ... And that's how I got on the
Town.
(Retired employee)

Well, what really brought it to a head
was ... it came to a Christmas time ...
I'd been quite busy all year and yet
I'd very little to go and buy Christmas
presents for my family. I'd a boy and
a girl, and I felt ... Well, it wasn't
fair to the family that I should be
working all these hours with very little
to show for it. When I was working for
a boss, I knew exactly what money I'd
be earning. Therefore, I approached
the council and I'd an interview with
the manager, it was Mr. (x) at that time,
and I got a start more or less right
away with them.
(Worker, aged 57 years)

As Table 4.3 shows, men often answered the
question about why they had gone to work for the
council in terms of precipitating factors, i.e.
something had happened to their previous jobs, and
they were without work. The council happened to be
'taking on' when other employers were not; so they
went to work there, and came to value the security.

What took you to the council 25
years ago?

There was very little work at the time
and I was ... there wasn't much work
in the building at that time.

When the building trade picked up
again were you tempted to leave?

Well, sometimes you were, really.
But I think I was just as well where
I was because there was more security

there than doing jobs where maybe, when
you were finished, you were laid off,
and you'd to wait until ... In the
painting trade there was a lot of
unemployment in the wintertime. They'd
try and keep you working in the council,
you see.
(Retired employee)

Table 4.3

Building and Works Department sample: reasons for
going to work with the council (*)

	Retired men		Current workers		All men	
	No.	Per cent	No.	Per cent	No.	Per cent
Redundant from previous job and council were 'taking on'	12	33.3	6	37.5	18	34.6
Pay levels at the council	0	0	0	0	0	0
Security/pay stabilisation	16	44.4	8	50.0	24	46.2
Pension	2	5.6	1	6.3	3	5.8
Other	6	16.7	1	6.3	7	13.5
Totals	36	100.0	16	100.1	52	100.1

(*) refers to last or current period of employment

   Marginally more often, though, security and pay
stabilisation were considerations that directed
their application for work with the local authority.
Council wages were not attractive in comparison
with the private sector, but they had a compensating
regularity which became important to men as they
moved into middle age and late working life.

   With the council you knew your pay was
coming in every week irrespective of the
weather or such as that. The wage was
maybe not as big as you were making

outside, but you knew you were going to
get a specific wage for 52 weeks a year.
That made a big difference.
(Worker, aged 56 years)

No men spoke of the wages offered by the council
as any kind of inducement for seeking employment
there; a regular wage packet was more important
than the wage level. This also overshadowed the
prospect of an occupational pension. Younger men
did not appear to give this aspect of security much
thought, and for older men it would not amount to
much because there were few years of service
possible before retirement.

I knew it would be superannuated, which
was contributory, you see. I knew all
about that, but I didn't really think
much about it because that was thirteen
years on. I didn't do it to get superannuated. I'd enough confidence in
what I was doing that I could get work.
I always had up to then.
(Retired employee)

Paradoxically, the pension scheme was of great
importance to the department's administrators when
interviewing applicants, because it was something
that few private building firms offered. While it
was an important inducement, it was not necessarily
an easy one to 'sell' to prospective employees.

The younger ones ... I don't think it
even registers. The thing about it is -
we're a little biased here - because
we are tied with these rates. We can't
offer the external contractor's rates.
We would raise that with them. We
would raise the fact because we
consider that the superannuation scheme
is very much a 'plus' in our employment
contract. While they wouldn't raise
it we would, because we want them.
They say, 'If I go to Wimpey I would get
another £10 a week.' Now, in purely
financial terms it's quite obvious that
they have to think about it ... We find
this all the time. Even with existing
staff, we're losing people because they
decide that they're more interested in the
immediate gratification than the deferred

pension scheme.
(Official, Building and Works Department)

At the time of the research, the local labour
market was a healthy one for building trades workers.
While, nationally, there was a slump in the demand
for such workers which, arguably, was a factor in the
development of DLO legislation, and the nature of
central government directives (Flynn and Walsh,
1982); the demand locally was strong. Recent
building activity in Aberdeen had meant a buoyant
market for local tradesmen (14), as it was cheaper
for large national contractors to 'take on' in the
area, and so avoid the additional expenses involved
in bringing workers from their home base. While
the demand for different trades varied (15),
overall demand was strong enough to present the
department with a persistent problem.

> Aberdeen, as far as tradesmen are
> concerned, is a very special case ...
> lots and lots of vacancies. So you
> could say to me, if you were a joiner,
> and you didn't like us, 'Sod you, I'm
> going somewhere else.' And you can
> go and get a job. Now, if you go out-
> side Aberdeen ... you go to Peterhead ...
> you can't do that.
> (Official, Building and Works Department)

This situation worked to the advantage of middle
aged and older men, giving them a value which in
most of Britain they would not have.

> Well, actually, we do take them on
> though it depends on their trade ...
> The older man ... might be referred
> for a medical. If he's in sound
> health we would take him on, but that's
> not being benevolent, that's dictated
> by the labour market. Now, if we
> were talking about the same situation
> down south, you wouldn't look at him.
> You'd go for somebody newly qualified,
> or somebody a little bit younger.
> (Official, Building and Works Department)

Middle-aged and older men who came to the department at times of difficulty in the industry, or in
the wake of individual employment terminations,
tended to stay and value the security that this
employment offered. The use of the 'Town' as a

distress employer, or as an employer in middle age
and late working life when job security could no
longer be framed in terms of sequential employment,
meant that service levels among those interviewed
were relatively low - certainly in comparison with
Stoneywood Mill.

Table 4.4

Building and Works Department sample: years of
service completed at retirement or interview (*)

	Retired men		Current workers		All men	
	No.	Per cent	No.	Per cent	No.	Per cent
10 years or less	7	19.4	2	12.5	9	17.3
11-20 years	8	22.2	5	31.3	13	25.0
21-30 years	14	38.9	8	50.0	22	42.3
31 + years	7	19.4	1	6.3	8	15.4
Totals	36	99.9	16	100.1	52	100.0

(*) Refers to last or current period of employment.

   Unlike Stoneywood Mill which had a very limited
pattern of ingress in mid-to-late working life, the
Building and Works Department was largely characterised by such moves. In an industry noted for its
employment insecurity, the department had offered
security attractive to men past their first flush
of youth. The work situation there was pressured,
to some extent, by the incentive bonus scheme but,
until recently, the department had been outside the
competitive environment of private sector firms.
Equally, the type of work - basically that of
jobbing builders - had utilised their skills and
experience and placed rather less emphasis on sheer
physical strength and speed. However, even
building work of this kind remains more demanding
than most jobs, so even minor health failure or
industrial senescence could have serious employment
consequences. With local labour market difficulties, departmental management placed a high value on
fit and healthy older workers but, as outlined in
the next chapter, there were few light work

opportunities for those who did not match up to the demands.

NOTES

(1)   Gouldner (1954) uses the term 'indulgency
       pattern' in reference to the diplomatic
       blindness of the former manager of a gypsum
       plant in respect of misuse of time and
       materials. The term is used here, not in
       the sense, of connivance with deviance, but
       to describe managerial tolerance of older
       workers' diminished utility.
(2)   There are many terms used to describe
       directly-employed labour for local authority
       construction, repair and maintenance work.
       Tilley (1976) cites direct labour
       organisation, direct works, public works,
       building works and construction services as
       just some of the titles used. The term
       currently in vogue is direct labour
       organisation (DLO).
(3)   Standard performance is defined as ... 'the
       rate of output which qualified workers will
       naturally achieve without over-exertion as
       an average over the working day or shift
       provided they adhere to the specified method
       and provided they are motivated to apply
       themselves to their work. This performance
       is denoted as 100 on the standard rating and
       performance scales.' (International Labour
       Office, 1969, p. 259).
(4)   Tilley (1976) notes that the Bains Report
       (The New Local Authorities: Management and
       Structure, 1972) which was the management
       blueprint for reorganisation in England and
       Wales, did not even mention direct labour
       building as a matter for the new authorities
       to consider. The equivalent management
       document for Scotland, the Paterson Report
       (The New Scottish Local Authorities:
       Organisation and Management Structure, 1973)
       did, however, consider property maintenance.
(5)   Meadows (1981) notes that the Conservative
       Party placed particular emphasis on local
       government activities in its manifesto for
       the 1979 election - clearly promoting the
       view that they were subordinate to the
       requirements of central government.

(6)   The Local Government Planning and Land Act
        (1980) was implemented on 1 April 1981 in
        England and Wales, and on 1 April 1982 in
        Scotland.

(7)   Section 10 of the Local Government Planning
        and Land Act (1980) distinguishes the
        following categories of work for accountancy
        purposes; (a) general highway work
        (construction and maintenance); (b) works
        of new construction and maintenance above
        £50,000 in value; (c) works of new
        construction below £50,000 in value; and
        (d) works of maintenance.

(8)   Section 16 of the Local Government Planning
        and Land Act (1980) requires authorities to
        show in respect of each financial year ...
        'such positive rate of return on the capital
        employed for the purpose of carrying out
        the work as the Secretary of State may
        direct.'

(9)   Section 9 of the Local Government Planning
        and Land Act (1980) forbids local authorities
        to undertake functional work (i.e. construct-
        ion or maintenance work), except where they
        have first obtained a written statement of
        costs from the DLO or, as directed by the
        Secretary of State, the authority has
        invited tenders for the work.

(10)   For discussion of DLO reaction to the
        legislation in Scotland see ADLO (Association
        of Direct Labour Organisations) News
        September 1982; November 1983.

(11)   Flynn, Walsh and Halford (1983) note new
        regulations to this effect applying in
        England and Wales from 1 October 1983. Works
        Committee minutes (Minutes of the City of
        Aberdeen District Council, 17 October 1983,
        p. 1061) revealed that, unless it could be
        demonstrated to Scottish Office Ministers
        that DLOs were already 'competing for a
        sufficient proportion of their work' the
        competition regulations that applied in
        England and Wales as from 1 October 1983
        would apply in Scotland on 1 April 1984.
        The demonstration was, presumably,
        unconvincing because the Local Government
        (Direct Labour Organisations) (Competition)
        (Scotland) Regulations (1984) confirmed the
        parallel with England and Wales. However,
        some respite was allowed for works of

minor maintenance in transitional arrangements for the period 1 April 1984 to 31 March 1985.

The 1984 regulations, the latest in a series of ever-tighter competition directives, required that, in respect of maintenance work, jobs valued at £10,000 or more had to be submitted for competition. For jobs valued at less than £10,000, 60 per cent of the work had to be submitted to competition, or put out to contract. While there was a higher threshold (£50,000) for new construction, the percentage tendering requirement was similar (City of Aberdeen District Council, September 1985).

(12)   At the Institute of Management Services Conference ('Direct Labour Organisations - Two Years On', Glasgow, 22 February 1984), Brian Gallagher, Director of Building Works, Glasgow District Council, suggested that the hidden agenda of the 1980 Act was, in fact, to reduce levels of employment in the public sector building industry.

(13)   It was noted (City of Aberdeen District Council, September 1983, p. 15) that during the 1982-3 financial year ... 'a total of 97,308 separate work orders were received of which 95,944 were completed. The remaining 1,364 (1.4 per cent) were carried forward into the current ... [1983-4] ... financial year.'

(14)   Although not an exhaustive set of local statistics, it was reported by the Job Centre in Aberdeen that in the period January 1983 to January 1984, there had been ... 'a total of 254 vacancies notified for joiners and 25 for masons/bricklayers'. Further ... 'at present we have vacancies for 31 joiners, 6 masons/bricklayers, 6 plasterers, 7 slaters and 7 plumbers; and with building firms just re-starting after the New Year holidays, it is anticipated that demand for those types of workers will increase.' (Extracts from correspondence with Job Centre, Aberdeen, 9 January 1984).

(15)   It was reported that 224 houses in the city were standing empty awaiting work by the Building and Works Department. The Depute

Director was attributed with the words ...
'I just can't get painters' (Evening
Express, 10 September 1980).

5 Late working life with the 'Town'

INTRODUCTION

Late working life with the 'Town' had been affected
by a number of changes in the organisation and
operation of local government. Following implementation of the Local Government (Scotland) Act
1973 in 1975, certain categories of work were lost
to men who had previously been employed by the City
of Aberdeen Corporation. This had some effect in
terms of the kind of work available - particularly
important in poor weather. However, in the wake of
regionalisation, there emerged a more distinct
emphasis on operational efficiency. At a local
level, this underwrote decentralisation and
administrative restructuring and caused problems
for those older men who had foreman or sub-foreman
status. Failure to obtain one of the new posts
meant a choice between demotion and early retirement, with the latter having much to offer for men
in this difficult situation. The loss of trade
foremen had implications for other older workers as
explained later in this chapter.

   The most important expression of concern over
efficiency in DLOs was, however, contained in Part
III of the Local Government Planning and Land Act

1980. This piece of legislation established a
framework of performance criteria seeking to ensure
that they were financially competitive with the
private sector building industry. The introduction
of 'competitiveness' into a previously uncompetitive
work environment was probably the most profound
change of all although, at the time of the research,
the effects were only just starting to be felt.
While other changes, even the 1973 Act, left a
substantial workload for the department, the most
recent central government directives relating to
the 1980 Act put the future workload in question.
If private firms successfully compete against the
department for local authority repair and maintenance work, then general or sectional demanning might
well proceed further than has already been
suggested.

As an undercurrent, but congruent with the formal
aims of these organisational changes, work was
tensioned by an incentive bonus scheme. 'Bonus' and
'work study' were important talismen in the accounts
of late working life. Although the bonus scheme
predated even local government reorganisation, it
was the main mechanism used by the administration to
relate day-to-day working practices to overall
performance targets. While it drew a fair degree of
adverse comment from older workers and retirees, it
seemed destined to occupy an increasingly important
role as competitiveness with private building firms
dominated the thoughts of management.

Table 5.1

Current workers: views on the prospect
of continuing with present job to 65 years

	No.	Per cent
Did not think it possible	3	18.8
No problems envisaged	8	50.0
Not sure, or a positive response qualified in terms of health or changes in the work situation	5	31.3
Totals	16	100.1

When older workers were asked if they thought they would be able to carry on working in their present job until they were 65 years, they demonstrated perspectives shaped by their currently strong position in this enclave of the local labour market rather than the uncertainties posed by the 1980 Act. Interestingly, the negative responses were not occasioned by certainty that jobs would not last that long, and there would be no opportunity to work to the state pensionable age. Rather, the three men concerned had concluded that it would be better for them to retire early. Two thought that they would have retired of their own volition before they reached 65 years. This they judged to be an appropriate perspective given what they saw as a deteriorating work situation, not actually inducing fears of redundancy or enforced early retirement, but already changing their feelings towards their jobs. Neither stressed the positive potential of life in retirement, except as a release from their present dissatisfactions.

Have you thought much about retirement?

Quite a lot, aye. It can't come quick enough. It's like wishing your life away, but ... in fact, I've seriously been thinking of looking into this early retiral ... you know, at sixty-two.

The Job Release Scheme?

If things continue as they are, I might seriously consider that.

Has anything in particular made you think about retirement?

Just the set-up now, the way things are going. There's no harmony in the work, or nothing now, you know. The workforce is alright together ... working together ... but I think it's the management level that's at fault, you know.
(Worker, aged 61 years)

The third man had gone one step further and was set to retire, under the Job Release Scheme, one month after the interview. He shared the disenchantment of the other two men.

The intermediate response category - a 'qualified optimism' and 'not sure' - were distinguishable in the degree and type of uncertainty. Some said they were not sure, because of existing health problems, whether they would still be working at 65 years. Others qualified their positive response by reference to the ceteris paribus proviso, i.e. they were optimistic provided that job circumstances or health did not alter dramatically. Only one suggested that redundancy in his section might bring forward his retirement.

> It's changed immensely. As a matter of fact, it's on its way out, I think. I doubt very much if I'll ... I give it three years. They'll bring in private enterprise, you know. I heard that they're phasing out the slaters. I don't know if there's any truth in it. We was told that the work they have up here for the slaters ... once it's finished, that's the slaters finished ... I think if we got rid of Maggie Thatcher things might settle down. Nine out of ten of the chaps there are saying, 'If we manage to hang on to our jobs until she gets out of power, we might manage to hang on to our jobs; but failing that ...'
> (Worker, aged 56 years)

Overall, there were much higher levels of optimism than had been the case at Stoneywood Mill. In the Building and Works Department, half the current workers interviewed were confident of their continued employment prospects. At the time of the interviews, older workers still grounded their perspectives in the fact that they had a certain scarcity value, and their skills and experience were not invalidated. It was rare to find pessimism based on impending competition with the private sector.

THE DECLINE IN WORK ABILITY

When older council workers were asked if they thought that a man's work deteriorated with age, relatively few of them gave unqualified agreement. One man who did even related his move to the council, 11 years earlier, to the growing realisation that he needed to get lighter work.

> ... beginning to slow up ... beginning to
> feel all your aches and pains, and things
> like that. That was one of the main
> reasons why I left (X), because when you
> swing a hammer for 17 years and you hit
> nothing but steel, your joints go all
> to hell ...
> (Worker, aged 56 years)

More often, though, there was an agreement qualified with reference to the way older workers compen-
sated for their physical slowing down.

> I've certainly slowed up as far as the time
> I can take to do a job, but the older you
> get, very often the quicker you can come up
> with the answer of what's causing faults, and
> how to prevent them. You known that by
> experience; the time that you've been working
> on these, you can put your finger on things
> a lot quicker than the younger chaps do.
> (Worker, aged 57 years)

> I would think that as you get older, you
> see, you learn a lot of 'quirks', and
> things about jobs. You can make it easier
> for yourself, or you can make it hard, but
> I don't think I could compete with young
> people 'outside' now, in the building
> trade, because to all intents and purposes,
> it's just a rat-race now, you know.
> (Worker, aged 61 years)

Table 5.2

Current workers: reactions to the
idea that a man's work deteriorates with age

	No.	Per cent
Unqualified agreement, or agreement qualified with reference to compensatory characteristics	7	43.8
Unqualified rejection, or rejection qualified with reference to compensatory characteristics	9	56.3
Totals	16	100.1

Denials were voiced because older men generalised from personal inapplicability or because experience, in their view, actually made older workers better than younger men. In addition, some denials focussed on the falsity of the idea given that the bonus system required performance to be maintained irrespective of age.

No, I would say quite the reverse actually. I can think of plenty of examples of that in our place. Younger men - they're not getting the chance, I'll not condemn them out-of-hand - but they don't get the same chance to learn the trade that we did, you know. There's too many short cuts and, well, there's not the skill called for nowadays, I don't think. But apart from that their attitude is a bit different from ours, I think. Once again, I'm not condemning all young lads, because there's a lot of good young lads, but there's some who couldn't care less and their job is suffering from that attitude. You know, that's an attitude to life they have so, naturally, it's taken into their work. It's funny you should ask this because just the other day, the supervisor, he said, 'Well, you're retiring shortly, and I'll tell you this and I'm not trying to turn your head or anything like that.' I said, 'You're a bit late for that.' And he said, 'We don't have many conscientious men that you can leave to do a job and you know there's no comebacks.' No, I think if it's inbred in you, I don't think your work should deteriorate unless your health's deteriorating, and then that would maybe show up in your work ... We've a few old boys and they've all the same attitude as I have. I would say that they're more dependable time-wise. I mean, there's very few of the old boys you see coming in late. If they do, it's few and far between. It's maybe an isolated case - very seldom - always on time, but I can't say the same about younger lads now. (Worker, aged 64 years)

The response profile was interesting in its rein-forcement of the point that perception of one's working ability is grounded in the structural

circumstances of late working life. In their work
with the council, older men were successfully able
to compete with younger men because their experience
did count. Jobbing repairs and maintenance, while
sometimes heavy, did not allow younger men the kind
of competitive advantage they would have had in
'new' construction work.

To some extent it might be argued that measured
performance served a useful purpose for older men as
they had weekly feed-back to suggest that their work
performance was within acceptable limits. None of
the men, however, suggested the system had this kind
of value, although the point did emerge in a more
oblique form when denials cited the bonus scheme.

> I don't think so, if it's an interesting
> job he can carry it out ... quite well.
> I can only speak from the experience that
> I've had. I've found younger men don't
> work any faster. As you're well aware,
> we have a bonus set-up. The time's the
> same whatever you are - twenty or sixty -
> the time's the same. There's no allow-
> ances made for age, or ill-health. It's
> just the same, and if you can't do it
> in that time there's an inquiry.
> (Worker, aged 56 years)

The circumstances of their work were not conducive
to extreme age-consciousness, and related perceptions of mental and physical decline. This is not
to say that age was ignored, it was for many of them
associated with greater experience, but it failed
to become a 'master trait' in work identity. This
is illustrated in Table 5.3, where it is clear that
few of these older men believed that they were a
separate category of worker.

Although it was seldom denied that ageing brought
few benefits in this line of work, perceptions of
the decline in work ability were limited by the
organisational factors that required and ensured
performance comparable with younger men. It was
noteworthy that even within the denial of 'older
worker' categorisation, responses focussed on a
general lack of age consciousness or the ability
to 'manage' jobs rather than the situational
anaesthesia of interaction with younger people
allowing one to forget the 'realities of one's age'.

Table 5.3

Current workers: extent to which they thought of themselves as being in a different category to other workers

	No.	Per cent
Considered themselves to be in a different category	1	6.3
Did not consider themselves to be in a different category	15	93.8
Totals	16	100.1

In summary, therefore, older employees demonstrated only a very circumscribed belief in age-related decline. The structural circumstances of their work facilitated a robust, but not entirely atemporal self-image. Age took on more of an 'auxiliary' character in this particular work setting.

CHANGING JOBS IN LATE WORKING LIFE

While the peculiarities of the local labour market for building trades workers gave older applicants a better chance of employment with the department than would otherwise have been the case, most of the retirees and current employees interviewed had entered local authority service at less than 54 years. Only 6 (16.7 per cent) of the 36 retirees, and 2 (12.5 per cent) of the current workers had been 'late entrants'.

While employment conditions in the private sector were often arduous, and gave advantage to youth, late entrants to the department were not distinguished by 'entry accounts' that centred on incipient decline. All had been out of work, or under notice, immediately before their move to the council.

I was made redundant when I was sixty, by (A), but previous to that (A) had bought the firm I was with, which was (B). Now, what I think ... we should have got the

chance from (B) to take our redundancy,
but we never. We were sold lock, stock
and barrel like a lot of cattle to (A),
and (A) ... decided they didn't want us.
So they made us redundant. Then I was
fortunate enough to get a job with
Aberdeen District Council ...

How did you feel being made redundant at
sixty?

... it came right out of the blue, you
know. You're just made redundant. In
fact I've got a bit of paper. I've just
looked out these things because you were
coming ... This is the bit of paper, like.
It really had a traumatic effect on me.
I'll tell you ... working there since ...
1955? ... That's quite a while; and I
was foreman joiner as you see there.

(LATER) There were another two joiners,
younger than me, and they said, 'We're
going to the District Council to get
these forms.' Just like that, 'Do you
want me to get one?' I said, 'Aye, get
one for me.' And so, I filled it in,
and they filled it in. I never saw anybody, they handed it back, and I got a
start after the holidays, you see.
However, they went to (C), the builders,
one of the biggest builders in Aberdeen.
They went to (C) because there was more
pay and bonus, you know, but I wasn't
interested by this time. I wasn't
interested.
(Retired employee)

A small proportion of both current and retired
workers had, therefore, changed employers in late
working life; but job changing was not limited to
late entry. Internal labour mobility meant that
an additional 9 (25 per cent) of the 36 retirees,
and 2 (12.5 per cent) of the 16 current workers
did not have the same job at retirement, or interview, as at 54 years. Taking late entry and
internal transfers together, job changing was a
feature of the late working lives of 34.6 per cent
of all respondents.

As shown in Table 5.4, though, there was a

noticeable, but not statistically significant, difference between current workers and retirees in the extent of job changing in late working life. This difference could, perhaps, be explained as a result of comparing complete and incomplete work histories. However, as 80 per cent of the retirees who had changed jobs in late working life had last changed jobs within 5 years of their retirement, and 62.5 per cent of the current workers interviewed were 60 years or over, a substantial pattern of job changing would have to develop if the current workers were ever to match the retirees. This would appear unlikely.

Table 5.4

Retired and current workers: extent of job changing between 54 years and retirement or interview

	Retired men		Current workers		All men	
	No.	per cent	No.	Per cent	No.	Per cent
Same job at 54 yrs. as at retirement or interview	21	58.3	13	81.3	34	65.4
Changed jobs at least once in that period	15	41.7	3	18.8	18	34.6
Totals	36	100.0	16	100.1	52	100.0

(X^2 = 1.6, Yates' Correction applied, 1 deg. f., not significant at 0.05 level)

There were several factors which mitigated against internal redeployment and, arguably, the influence of these factors was greater for current workers than it had been for retirees. The division of labour within the department was such that there were few ancillary roles to which ageing, or ailing, manual workers could be transferred. In mid-1983, for example, only 20 men were engaged in storekeeper/yardman/watchman-type roles as opposed to 373 in mainstream trade roles (1). The latter out-numbered the former by nearly 19 to 1, so

relatively few older manual workers could finish
their working lives in this sort of ancillary
capacity. Equally, the department needed trade
personnel (2). Although there was differential
demand, there was little reason for the department
to move older men to tasks beyond the customary
limits of a particular trade. Further, it is deb-
atable whether transfer to ancillary roles would
have been attractive to men who had, for several
decades, organised their identitities around work
in a particular craft and had, accordingly, been
paid at the trade rate. Transfers of this kind
were extremely rare. Taking retirees and current
workers together, only 2 men moved from trade to
ancillary roles. Most internal job changing was
accomplished <u>within</u> trade roles; the older men
retaining their trade status even if the work they
did was different. However, redeployment of this
sort was informal and required the assistance of
supervisory personnel. Trade foremen had been
important in 'fixing' changes in job content for
those who were industrially senescent, or were
experiencing health difficulty.

Table 5.5

Retired and current workers: reasons for last or
only job change in late working life

	Retired men		Current workers		All men	
	No.	Per cent	No.	Per cent	No.	Per cent
Out of work in the private sector (*)	6	40.0	1	33.3	7	38.9
Poor health	5	33.3	0	0	5	27.8
Reorganisation	0	0	1	33.3	1	5.6
Sought inside work	0	0	1	33.3	1	5.6
Discretionary redeployment	3	20.0	0	0	3	16.7
Promotion	1	6.7	0	0	1	5.6
Totals	15	100.0	3	99.9	18	100.2

(*) Includes 1 retired employee who was under
    notice in his previous job

The administrative role of trade foremen, prior
to restructuring in 1981, put them in the position
of being able to match man and job. While this
power was important to workers at any age, in the
aftermath of illness or injury, it was particularly
so in later years when difficulties might prove
more intractable, and require permanent or regular
placement of a worker in a less-demanding aspect
of the work.

> You were asking earlier on about the work.
> Well, dismantling one machine ... I had
> one chap that did hurt his back. He was
> off work a few days and then he went
> back and, until he felt fit, I kept him
> on as light duties as I possible could
> which was just mainly maintenance work
> where he had no lifting at all to do.
> (Worker, aged 57 years)

> The last four or five years before my
> retirement I was working in the depot, at
> Kittybrewster and Jasmine Terrace. I was
> doing most of the preparation, priming
> new doors. glazing new doors, and all the
> priming work. And I was also 'coaching on'
> the apprentices, putting them through ...
> keeping them up with a little paper
> hanging and such, you know.

> What brought that about?

> Well, what actually happened was that I
> took arthritis in my knee, and the foreman
> that was in charge at the time ... I spoke
> to him about it, and the chap that was
> working in the yard retired, and he said,
> 'Ach, you can come into the yard and work.'
> So that's what happened. It was a question
> of a bad knee for the climbing and such
> like.
> (Retired employee)

> I would say that the foremen I've worked
> under have been pretty fair that way.
> That's one thing I can't complain an
> awful lot about. I've been pretty lucky
> that way with good foremen, you know.
> (Worker, aged 56 years)

Multi-trade supervisors, in contrast, were not
only operating at 'one step removed' from day-to-

day working practices in specific trades, but were part of an administration charged with the task of demonstrating competitiveness and efficiency to satisfy the requirements of the Local Government Planning and Land Act (1980), and its associated performance directives.

> Not one bit, no. I've heard it said on a few occasions ... 'If you're not fit for the job, get out' ... more or less, you know what I mean. That's the attitude. You're required to do a job and that's it. It might have been ... a year or two back when the foremen and all the rest were there, you know, but not now. I mean, we have no foremen ...
> (Worker, aged 61 years)

> They make no difference. You're expected to do the same as what the younger person does, you see. It doesn't matter how old you are.
> (Worker, aged 62 years)

There were, therefore, difficulties in the acquisition of light work <u>within</u> the department. The retirees pattern of late working life job changing had been considerably enchanced by 'late entry'. In fact, as Table 5.5 shows, 40 per cent of their job changing activity was attributable to this. It is interesting to speculate on the situation of these late entrants had they not had the advantage of a 'peculiar' local labour market. Undoubtedly, some would have had to enter retirement via unemployment as, at some stage, competition in the private sector with younger men would have proved unequal. As it was, late entry and internal job changing had the effect of extending late working lives, for 66.7 per cent of the men who retired at 65 years changed their jobs at some point in the preceding 11 years compared with 29.2 per cent of those who retired before that age. The effect was evident also in the average ages at retirement. For all retirees, the mean average was 61.9 years but for non-changers it was 60.9 years, and for job changers it was 63.3 years.

Wider opportunities for internal job changing would not have forestalled early retirement for <u>all</u> early retirees. Displaced foremen, for example, experiencing early retirement as disguised redundancy could not have been helped in this way.

Also, at the point of retirement, the availability of light work would not have helped many health retirees as they were declared totally unfit. However, given lighter work earlier in late working life, the situation might, in some cases, have been quite different. Even with the health circumstances that prevailed at retirement, 21.4 per cent of health retirees had re-engaged in the labour market.

THE NATURE OF THE JOB CHANGES

Analysis of alterations to the content of work brought about by late working life job changing differs from that for Stoneywood Mill on two points. First, it should be noted that late entrants are fully included in job changer figures. In the parallel analysis for Stoneywood Mill, the small number of men in this category were not included in data on jobs at 54 years. In contrast with the mill, late entrants to the department still engaged in the same occupation although the exact content of their work might well have been different. The circumstances of these two groups of late entrants were thought sufficiently different to warrant this procedural variation. Second, because this organisational context was quite unlike the mill, discussion centres on a reduced and modified range of light work features. 'Work pattern' does not apply because there was no shift work in the department, and 'functional role' is replaced by 'work location' as internal job changing nearly always took place within trade roles although the location of the work was, in some instances, different. Equally, as work in the department was varied, 'job pace' is not considered as a feature. Reference is, however, made to work study and the incentive scheme towards the end of the chapter, as it was a feature of manual work there irrespective of job changing.

(a) Physical effort

Although repair and maintenance work done by the department's manual employees tended to be lighter in its physical effort requirements than new construction work elsewhere, building activities were often arduous. At 54 years, 72.2 per cent of all retirees had been engaged in work they rated as always/mostly heavy or having mixed physical demands.

> Yes, well, you got your job and you went
> out to it, and it was up to you, you
> know. You had to ... I mean, if you'd
> have been too long they'd have been down
> to talk to you ... and then they had a
> bonus scheme too, you see. If you did
> it in a certain time you got so much.
> If you did it a wee bit quicker, you got
> so much more, you know what I mean. I
> found that a terrible lot easier. It
> was more repair work, that's what I mean
> by saying it was easier. Instead of having
> to plaster a whole house, you was only
> doing a repair job, you know. Then by
> the time you packed your stuff, and
> went away to another one, you'd had a
> bit of a rest, you know.
> (Retired employee)

Table 5.6

Retired men: comparison of physical effort required by jobs at retirement

	Job changers at retirement		Non changers at retirement		All men at retirement	
	No.	Per cent	No.	Per cent	No.	Per cent
Light/mostly light work	10	66.7	8	38.1	18	50.0
Always/mostly heavy or mixed physical demands	5	33.3	13	61.9	18	50.0
Totals	15	100.0	21	100.0	36	100.0

(not significant at 0.05 level)

As compared with subsequent non-changers at that age, those who changed their jobs through internal redeployment or late entry, were marginally less likely to have the lightest kind of work. As Figure 5.1 illustrates, only 13.3 per cent of

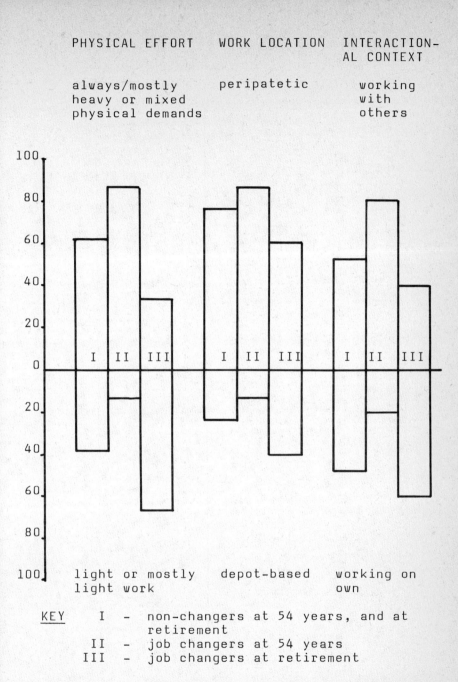

PHYSICAL EFFORT   WORK LOCATION   INTERACTION-
                                    AL CONTEXT

always/mostly   peripatetic   working
heavy or mixed   with
physical demands   others

light or mostly   depot-based   working on
light work   own

KEY   I - non-changers at 54 years, and at
               retirement
        II - job changers at 54 years
       III - job changers at retirement

Figure 5.1 Retired men: comparison of jobs
            at 54 years and at retirement

135

Table 5.7

Retired and current workers: comparisons of physical effort requirements at 54 years and at retirement or interview

| | Retired men | | | | Current workers | | | |
| | At 54 years | | At retirement | | At 54 years | | At interview | |
	No.	Per cent	No.	Per cent	No.	Per cent	No.	Per cent
Light/mostly light work	10	27.8	18	50.0	6	37.5	7	43.8
Mixed demands	16	44.4	8	22.2	7	43.8	7	43.8
Always/mostly heavy	10	27.8	10	27.8	3	18.8	2	12.5
Totals	36	100.0	36	100.0	16	100.1	16	100.1

these men were doing work they rated as 'light' or 'mostly light' at 54 years whereas, just before retirement, 66.7 per cent of their jobs had been described in this way. However, as shown in Table 5.6 above, the pattern of physical effort reduction was not sufficient to yield statistically signif- icant differences between job changers and non- changers at retirement.

It might have been anticipated that the dominant type of change in late working life would have been that of men moving from the heaviest kind of work to significantly lighter work. This, however, was not the case. The tendency was to move from work with mixed physical effort requirements to less strenuous work, as shown by the data on retired men in Table 5.7. One possible explanation for this finding might be that men who had the heaviest work at 54 years were among the first to retire. Their subsequently shorter period of late working life would have further reduced the scant likelihood for job changes that could have lightened their work. However, the men who reported the heaviest work at 54 years were not exceptional in terms of their age at retirement, the mean average being 61.6 years compared with 61.2 years for the lightest work and 62.5 years for mixed physical effort grading. In fact, a higher proportion retired at 65 years than was the case for men who had reported light or mixed demands for jobs at 54 years.

The explanation for the fairly static position of men who, at the 'start' of late working life, had the heaviest work would seem to be a function of the particular occupations represented in those responses. The vast majority of the men who eval- uated their work in this way were, arguably, in the most physically demanding building occupations - labourers, slaters and pipe-layers, for example. Within those occupational roles, the chances of securing job content changes resulting in a significant reduction of physical effort were probably much lower.

Current workers demonstrated a much weaker trend in the acquisition of physically lighter work. In fact, only 1 of the 3 job changers had secured lighter work by moving from a slater's job that he regarded as 'mostly heavy' to a stores job that was 'light work'. However, as shown in Table 5.7, retirees were more likely to have heavier gradings of work at the end of their organisational careers than current workers at the time of interview. Given what had happened to retirees, though, there was considerable _scope_ for reduction of physical effort from mixed demands to lighter work.

   Apart from the possible outcome of late entry, reducing work's physical demands in late working life at the department was primarily dependent on opportunities to secure changed job content within specific occupational roles. It could be argued that administrative restructuring, in conjunction with more stringent financial constraints, had contributed to a reduction in this kind of opport- unity and, consequently, in the possibility of gaining physically lighter work. The future would appear to offer early retirement, rather than lighter and more easily managed work, to those current workers who, in spite of their optimism for job continuity to the state pensionable age, come up against the problems of industrial senescence or ill-health.

(b) Work location

The bulk of the department's work was carried out away from the central and area depots. These were largely places to work _from_ rather than buildings to work _in_. Manual workers, in most trades, usually spent their working day 'out and about' repairing and maintaining the council's housing stock, using the depots only as a point of reference for materials and paperwork. A few jobs, however, were depot-based. Although supervisory work took them out to the actual work locations, supervisors and their foreman and sub-foreman predecessors, were based in depots. Below this administrative stratum, though, there were only a handful of men who identified their jobs with particular premises. The exceptions were mostly men engaged in prepar- ation work and materials handling for different trades, but one trade group, the blacksmiths, worked in the depot at Kittybrewster.

   Most men were, therefore, peripatetic in their everyday work. This granted them a degree of autonomy in the way they accomplished the jobs they were sent to do. The autonomy, however, was not absolute because, with larger jobs at least, a

chargehand would probably be present, and performance, on jobs of all sizes, had to be reconciled
with job tickets and daily work sheets. Administrative visits and 'comeback' from tenants were
additional limitations. What autonomy they had was,
in any case, counterbalanced by the fact that their
work had to be carried out in conditions that were
largely beyond the worker's control. Problems of
access, transport, site difficulties and the
weather were all salient detractions from the
benefits of having no fixed place of work.

One anomaly in the logic of decentralisation was
that while employees were nearer the source of
their workload, the actual transference of men and
materials from area depots to various parts of the
housing schemes proved a constant source of
aggravation. This applied primarily to men sent
out to deal with small repair jobs.

> Another thing as regards the Council;
> if I didn't have a motor car there's no
> way that I could have worked for them.
> Just no way! Imagine carrying a bag of
> tools around with you. We did all
> Mastrick ... everything you can see out
> there ... [points] ... and those multi-
> storeys over there. There's four ...
> there's seventy-two families in each ...
> each of those tenements, you know; and
> you've maybe to away up to the top.
> There was a fire once away at the top and
> ... we used to carry a stool. And that
> was the worst thing, I couldn't carry it.
> So if I didn't have a car I wouldn't
> have been ... and they didn't pay you
> for the car. You're not supposed to run
> a car. I mean, they didn't mind ...
> [laughs] ...

> They didn't provide vans?

> Well, there's one van for the whole depot
> down there. That's plumbers, electricians,
> masons, painters - the whole lot of them.
> About fifty men. So, if you've got to
> stand about and wait on a van, you'd
> stand all day.
> (Retired employee)

> To give you an idea, you have to carry
> the tools with you all the time. You see,

> I've no car. Some of the journeys I'd to
> walk ... say five minutes with my tools,
> walk back for my stool, then walk back
> for my timber. That's fifteen minutes
> gone! And by the time I'd spoken to the
> woman and explained the situation, that's
> twenty minutes passed and I haven't done
> a thing.
> (Retired employee)

As men got older it was sometimes the case that the
job itself began to present difficulties that would
have been more easily coped with when younger.

> Climbing in roof spaces, and that ... our
> job, we're invariably on our knees, or
> lying on our back under basins. All this
> new building and so forth ... plastics ...
> and the houses were going up at an
> enormous rate and I felt that sometimes
> the workmanship wasn't ... left a lot
> to be desired, you understand. You seemed
> to be folded up and lying on your back,
> and you're in the most awful positions.
> That's what's the trouble with my neck,
> you see. I felt the strain.
> (Retired employee)

> It was a cold job in the winter, mind,
> whatever age you were, and as you were
> getting older you felt the cold more than
> you did normally, you know. The younger
> you were in this job, the better. Well,
> I think you were anyway. It was a really
> good job in the summer as long as you were
> fit, like. But as I say, the winters ...
> and as you grow older it was a killer
> right enough. I mean, when I first went
> there nothing was any trouble to you but,
> as I said, when I was getting older you
> could feel it, you know. You could feel
> it in your body.
> (Retired employee)

Painters were particularly noteworthy not only for
their trade's susceptibility to bad weather, but
because regionalisation, in 1975, drastically
reduced the organisational possibilities for handling the problem. Before regionalisation, tradesmen
who had been engaged in external painterwork were
brought in during the really bad weather. There

140

was work to do in the various municipal buildings
under the control of the City of Aberdeen Corporation. This, in fact, was one of the attractions
of working with the 'Town' because it provided a
virtually unsupassed measure of work continuity for
the trade. The transfer of schools and clinics to
Grampian Region meant that there was little respite
for the District Council painters as the winter
tightened its grip (3).

> ... and in the wintertime, we weren't out
> in the cold. That's because there was
> always ... until this new Region, and that,
> started. That altered ... messed up ...
> the whole thing, you see. They took over
> different things but before that, as soon
> as it became bad weather we went into
> schools, nurseries, libraries, and that
> sort of thing. We were pretty comfortable
> all winter, you know. With some private
> firms you just had to stay outside. I've
> seen us outside in some pretty bad weather
> after the change-over. The last winter ...
> the last two winters I think ... I was out
> longer than I'd ever been before ... The
> Council's changed ... Course, you can't
> do a lot of painting if it's raining
> too bad, you know. You can do it when it's
> pretty cold, and there's not much action
> attached to it, you know. You're standing,
> 'cutting in' panes of glass ... It can be
> pretty deadly. You've got to run around
> the house now and again to get the
> circulation going ... [laughs] ...
> (Retired employee)

> They used to keep you outside as long as
> they possibly could, you see. If it was
> hard, like what it is now ... but as long
> as it wasn't raining they kept you out-
> side, you know. I've seen us go up at
> half-past-seven in the morning ... and
> there was aluminium ladders, you know ...
> and your fingers stuck to it, it was
> so cold. You were chipping ice off the
> windowsills, and everything, before you
> could really get started.
> (Retired employee)

Particularly in the 'outside' trades, men found
increasing difficulty with the combined effects of

Table 5.8

Retired and current workers: comparison of work location at 54 years and at retirement or interview

| | Retired men | | | | Current workers | | | |
| | At 54 years | | At retirement | | At 54 years | | At interview | |
	No.	Per cent	No.	Per cent	No.	Per cent	No.	Per cent
Peripatetic	29	80.6	25	69.4	11	68.8	10	62.5
Depot-based	7	19.4	11	30.6	5	31.3	6	37.5
Totals	36	100.0	36	100.0	16	100.1	16	100.0

age and organisational change. Roving work, which
confronted men with site and weather problems, lost
much of its appeal, but transfer to depot duties was
only a remote possibility.

Data presented in Table 5.8 shows that while there
was some movement from peripatetic work as a result
of late working life job changes, the tendency was
weak for retirees and for current workers. At 54
years, 80.6 per cent of all retirees had peripatetic
jobs and this had dropped to 69.4 per cent for last
jobs. As a result of late entry to the department
or internal redeployment 15 men had changed jobs,
but only 4 had become depot-based. Interestingly,
more current workers had been depot-based at 54
years, and at interview, than retired men at retirement. This, arguably, was a peculiarity of the
current worker sample because, in terms of the
acquisition of depot-based work after the age of 54
years, their experience was little different to
that of the retirees. Only one of the older men
currently employed by the department had secured a
depot job, and that on the basis of a formal
application for an advertised storeman post.

So while the move from peripatetic to depot-based
work may have been a desirable prospect to many of
the older men, especially if they could continue to
work within their trade, it was not a well-beaten
career path. As confirmed in Table 5.9, a significant change in work location patterns was not a
corollary of late working life job changing.

Table 5.9

Retired men: comparison of work location
at retirement

	Job changers at retirement		Non changers at retirement		All men at retirement	
	No.	Per cent	No.	Per cent	No.	Per cent
Peripatetic	9	60.0	16	76.2	25	69.4
Depot-based	6	40.0	5	23.8	11	30.6
Totals	15	100.0	21	100.0	36	100.0

(not significant at 0.05 level)

143

It is reasonable to suppose that the tightening of
working conditions following legislative change will
not make this kind of move any more available to
older men. If anything, opportunities will be
reduced in line with the less-sheltered circumstances of the private sector where ancillary and
peripheral trade tasks are likely to be seen as
unacceptable overheads. Sheltering, in the form of
changed work location, was both a minor pattern of
accommodation for older workers and one that
appeared vulnerable.

(c) Interactional context

The department's manual workers could find themselves working in teams, on their own, or with one
or two others depending on the size of the job in
hand. Planned maintenance involving refurbishment,
or major repair jobs, could involve squads of men.
Response maintenance and routine repair work often
involved single working, but sometimes it was
trade practice for two men to work together for
reasons of safety and convenience.

> With the lifts there are always two ...
> there's always the engineer and a mate,
> and they travel together. The idea for
> this is that you'd never be in a position
> where you find you're absolutely stuck ...
> you're jammed in.
> (Worker, aged 57 years)

One trade involved all three forms of deployment.
Painters worked in squads when they were redecor-
ating whole houses, whole streets or municipal
buildings. They worked singly, and in two's and
three's, on smaller-scale undertakings. There was
the theoretical possibility, then, for an older
man to move away from squad to single or small
group working, and there was certainly some movement of this kind. With other trades - plumbers,
electricians, joiners and masons for example - men
usually worked on their own, or in pairs. The
latter arrangement, because of the low ratio of
trade labourers to tradesmen, was normally
restricted to heavier and awkward work. There was,
therefore, less scope for changing the interactional context of work and reduction in physical
effort requirements by redeployment to smaller
jobs was the main option. At the other extreme,
scaffolders worked only in groups so, for older men

Table 5.10

Retired and current workers: comparisons of interactional context at 54 years and at retirement or interview

	Retired men				Current workers			
	At 54 years		At retire-ment		At 54 years		At inter-view	
	No.	Per cent	No.	Per cent	No.	Per cent	No.	Per cent
Working on own	13	36.1	19	52.8	6	37.5	7	43.8
Working with at least one other man	23	63.9	17	47.2	10	62.5	9	56.3
Totals	36	100.0	36	100.0	16	100.0	16	100.1

needing less-demanding work, the options were 'concealment' within the group or transfer away from the trade. The characteristics of this, and other 'rigorous' trades, precluded really effective redeployment. One scaffolder had, for example, been 'grounded' in his last year but, while he had thus been spared the hazards of climbing, he still rated his work as 'always heavy'.

There were, therefore, differential opportunities to move to solitary working within customary trade activities. This kind of change could, in any case, mean different things to different men. While it was characteristically associated with a move to lighter tasks, it was equally associated with detachment from a colleague group and, often, with a shift from collective to individual bonus calculations. The latter could, in fact, be counterproductive as some sheltering occurred in larger work groups.

> I couldn't always get on the ground all
> the time, you know. Sometimes you'd have
> to go and do second windows. In schools,
> you see, you'd be on a two-part extension
> ... going up and down all day. You found
> it quite difficult, but the chaps I was
> with were pretty good to me.
> (Retired employee)

It can be seen in Table 5.10 that, at 54 years, 36.1 per cent of retirees had worked on their own, but solitary working was a feature of 52.8 per cent of last jobs. A parallel but weaker trend was evident for current workers although, at 54 years, they had closely matched retirees at the same age.

Departmental workload and trade practices precluded a stronger pattern of change in interactional context and, from the data in Table 5.11, it can be seen that the differences between job changers and non-changers at retirement were not statistically significant.

146

Table 5.11

Retired men: comparison of interactional context at retirement

	Job changers at retirement		Non changers at retirement		All men at retirement	
	No.	Per cent	No.	Per cent	No.	Per cent
Working on own	9	60.0	10	47.6	19	52.8
Working with at least one other man	6	40.0	11	52.4	17	47.2
Totals	15	100.0	21	100.0	36	100.0

(not significant at 0.05 level)

LATE WORKING LIFE CAREERS

Job changing in late working life was much less
common here than had been the case at the paper
mill. In total, 41.7 per cent of the retirees, and
18.8 per cent of the current employees had changed
jobs at least once at, or after 54 years. These
figures were enhanced by the number of late
entrants who were taken on because there was a
strong market for tradesmen and the department was
in a relatively weak bargaining position. Late
entry accounted for 40 per cent of the job changing
among retirees and 66.7 per cent of that reported
by men still employed at the Building and Works
Department. If the effect of late entry on the
total extent of job changing was discounted there
was, by the standards of Stoneywood Mill, very
little evidence of modification to the work circumstances of older men. Some possibilities for
the redeployment of those who became industrially
senescent or suffered health impairment existed,
but they seldom became reality.

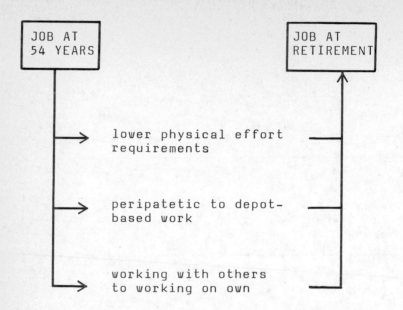

```
┌─────────────┐                      ┌─────────────┐
│ JOB AT      │                      │ JOB AT      │
│ 54 YEARS    │                      │ RETIREMENT  │
└─────────────┘                      └─────────────┘
       │                                    ▲
       │      ──▶  lower physical effort  ──│
       │           requirements             │
       │                                    │
       │      ──▶  peripatetic to depot-  ──│
       │           based work               │
       │                                    │
       └──────▶  working with others    ────┘
                  to working on own
```

Figure 5.2   Light work acquisition in the
              Building and Works Department

   Even when, as a result of late entry or internal
redeployment, older men had changed jobs, there
was relatively little clustering of the effects.
At most, there were 3 aspects of light work that
could be gained, but only 2 retirees managed
this - working on their own in a physically lighter
depot job. Altogether, 8 (53.3 per cent) of
retired job changers acquired 2 dimensions of
light work, but it was noteworthy that 5 men
(33.3 per cent) changed their jobs without any
change on the variables used in the analysis.
Their jobs before and after the change presented
much the same kind of demands. Further, among
current workers there were so few job changes that
the profile of light work acquisition must be
regarded as inconclusive. Given the age structure
of this group, though, one might have expected to
find more evidence not only of job changing, but
also of moves to less-demanding work.

Table 5.12

Retired and current workers: aspects of light work gained in the last or only job change in late working life

	Retired men		Current workers		All job changers	
	No.	Per cent	No.	Per cent	No.	Per cent
Two or more aspects of light work gained	8	53.3	1	33.3	9	50.0
One or no aspects of light work gained, or reversal involved	7	46.7	2	66.7	9	50.0
Totals	15	100.0	3	100.0	18	100.0

(not significant at 0.05 level)

Compared with the paper mill, there was a much less distinct pattern of job retrogression in the later years of work. Some men did change jobs but, using the terminology developed in Chapter 3, they did not embark on transition careers because less-demanding work was not gained as a result of the change, or changes. Taking congruent change on at least 2 aspects of light work to mark clear job retrogression, and to maintain comparability with the paper mill retirees, then 53.3 per cent of all retired job changers or 22.2 per cent of all retirees could be said to have ended their working lives on a transition career path. Mostly, careers conformed to the extension pattern where the job held at 54 years was also the job held at retirement, or the truncated extension pattern where job change, without the acquisition of light work, was followed by early retirement. Except for displaced foremen and sub-foremen, though, early retirements in the Building and Works Department were invariably brought about by poor health or as a response to industrial senescence. Neither condition could

149

be accommodated in the manner reported by Stoneywood
retirees where continued employment in late working
life was far less dependent on the health and fitness necessary to perform 'normal' work roles.

In fact, because manual work with the council was
continuously monitored in the operation of the
incentive bonus scheme, there was less ambiguity
possible in judgements of performance. For all
men, whether in light work posts or ordinary trade
roles, there was a 'standard performance' to
attain. Poor performance not only meant a reduction
in the bonus element of the wage, but brought
questions about the jobs on which inappropriate
times were returned. Neither outcome was particularly desirable so, while most men spoke out
against the performance measures involved in the
bonus scheme, none could really afford to ignore
them. This provided pressures in late working life
even if, as in the comment below, measured performance was regarded favourably.

> Everything you do is bonusable bar what
> they call unmeasured work ... but you've
> still got to attempt to make bonus and,
> well, if you go down to '70' performance,
> or maybe slightly less, you're not
> making bonus and they're down to see why.
> Against that, if you're up past '140',
> they want to know why. You've made too
> much! There's not much likelihood of
> that though. The time's are cut so fine
> now; once they got the hang of the thing,
> you know. They've got it to such a fine
> art that anybody who makes a '140' now
> should be going home on his hands and
> knees. I've no intention of doing that. I
> make quite good bonus actually. I'm
> always well over the '100', which is good;
> but some of the others don't make a '100'
> or, if they do, it's not much more. My
> average during the last couple of years
> is '106' - '108' performance, and that is
> considered fairly good by any standard
> in our work; but I'm a fairly steady
> worker. My attitude is, 'If you're
> going out to work you may as well work.'
> Irrespective of the fact that you should
> be. That doesn't enter some people's
> heads - the fact that you're being paid

and you should be working. Some spend as
much time trying to dodge work. That's
not my idea. I prefer having a job to do,
and doing it. I'm not trying to say I'm
over-conscientious, but I am conscientious
up to a point. I like to do a fair day's
work and I feel happier, you know. You
feel good within yourself. You've done a
fair day's work. You're happy with
yourself.
(Worker, aged 64 years)

  Mostly, though, performance measurement was
regarded as a problem. Accounts from older workers
and retirees revealed 3 interconnected criticisms;
first, times were generally 'tight'; second, the
resultant emphasis on speed was detrimental to the
quality of work; and thirdly, the system generated
a prodigious amount of paperwork.

  Times were sometimes regarded as 'tight' in an
absolute sense, i.e. the assignment of a precise
number of minutes to a craft operation was a bad
thing in itself. More often, however, it was the
combination of time plus site conditions that caused
concern.

  And another thing, the middle of the winter
  in a house ... a house that's been empty
  for three months is very, very cold and
  depressing. Sometimes the emulsion would
  freeze up. The stuff wouldn't dry; the
  paint wouldn't dry. Course, they don't
  accept that as an excuse in work study.
  They say, 'Well put in patent driers.'
  If you put in too much patent driers,
  the surface dries and underneath doesn't;
  and you get this 'gurning' effect.
  That's what causes that, incidentally,
  the different speed of drying in the
  surface of the paint.
  (Retired employee)

  Times are poor. You take a flat roof, a
  big flat roof, and you're scraping
  chuckies (*) off. Now you get nothing
  for scraping chuckies off. It's a hard
  job. You try scraping chuckies off that's
  been there for years. That was the worst
  part of the job ... The way they talk

151

it was easy.
(Retired employee)
(*) Chuckies, in this context, are small
    stones scattered on the felt surface
    of a flat roof to reduce the effect
    of solar heat on the bitumen.

With time as a paramount factor in a worker's
mind there was a frequently voiced belief that
craftsmanship was, perforce, becoming a secondary
consideration.

On maintenance you were doing, on average,
about eight jobs a day, you understand,
and quite candidly I felt you were working
on a job and you were thinking about
another job you were going to. You didn't
get on a job and say, 'Now, I'm going to
concentrate on this particular job.'
You were always thinking, 'Where am I
going to next?' We were on a bonus system
and you felt it, like, always at the
back of your mind.
(Retired employee)

I think your work suffered in a way. They
didn't give the same attention to the job.
It was more speed than quality of the job.
That's my opinion, anyway.
(Retired employee)

I can produce more work without bonus.
You put me on bonus I get excited; I
get panicky. Without bonus I can produce
more, but I did make bonus. The thing
was I was as good as the younger boys,
because I was 100 per cent ... Without
the strain I could do more, you know.
It's like racing one another.
(Retired employee)

Performance measurement relied heavily on a
precise and continuous flow of data. The paperwork
generated was made complex by the variability of
tasks.

You see, I might get a windowsill to
paint, to prime, and then would come
something else - a small window to
prime. It entailed piles of paperwork,
you know, to write out in detail what
I'd done; what material I had used for

152

each one. I had that to do. I had to
put down materials against each little
job that I did, you know. If you
painted a windowsill, you had to put in
a quantity - one gill of paint - and
such like against each job; and then
your job number and your time. To me ...
I thought it was all time-consuming
because the time I was using to write out
that bonus every day meant that I could
have been doing something else with the
paintbrush. Course, you get your extra
money for it; that's most important.
(Retired employee)

From the department's point of view, the quantification of time gave a measure of worker efficiency
and, by implication, organisational efficiency. For
older workers, though, it provided a source of
tension in late working life from which there was
no real respite. At best, the conditions under
which bonus was earned could be altered but, even
in the controlled conditions of depot work, bonus
and the constituent performance measurement were
organisational facts of life.

DISCUSSION

The Building and Works Department proved to be very
different from Stoneywood Mill as a context for late
working life. Both organisations were similar,
however, in the fact that changes had occurred
directly affecting older workers on the threshold
of their retirement.

The new department had emerged in the local government reorganisation of the mid-1970s with a
reduced range of work as compared with its City of
Aberdeen Corporation predecessor. The municipal
building work that was lost meant that manual
employees, particularly painters, had a reduced
supply of indoor work in poor weather. Although
the department still compared favourably with
private firms in the job security offered its
workers, there was no doubt that this particular
organisational change put a severe constraint on
one important benefit of council employment - a good
supply of indoor work in the harsh Scottish winters.

The department also underwent changes in the structure of its first-line management. Trade foremen, who had occupied a key position, were replaced by supervisors with multiple-trade responsibilities. This change affected more than those directly displaced for, within trade sections, foremen and sub-foremen had been instrumental in deploying men to tasks. This fact was important in the probability of transition careers within the limited set of light work possibilities.

Part III of the Local Government Planning and Land Act (1980), and its related performance directives, created conditions for a more competitive work environment and re-affirmed the logic of the incentive bonus scheme. Manual workers' performance was monitored, closely mirroring the financial scrutiny that increasingly beset management. Although, for older workers, this performance measurement provided a routine statement of their work ability, it was mostly viewed as a source of aggravation. One might expect that current employees will find this feature of local authority employment ever more obtrusive as the competitive requirements become stricter.

For most of the men interviewed, late working life did not involve the acquisition of light work, whether or not they changed jobs. The department had need of their skills and while, as an enclave in the local labour market for building trades workers, it might have offered a form of retrogression in its 'jobbing' style of operations, it could not effectively shelter those who subsequently became ill or industrially senescent. In those circumstances, it had little to offer other than early retirement. Few current employees had changed jobs in late working life, and it would seem highly likely that should their work ability be affected by poor health or industrial senescence, they will face the problem of reduced willingness to redeploy them into more suitable jobs in addition to the diminished capacity for such redeployment.

NOTES

(1)   The figures quoted exclude apprentices and supervisors. The actual ratio of trade to

154

ancillary roles, on this basis, was 18.7 to 1.

(2)   The demand provided by the Building and Works
       Department was largely restricted to qualified
       tradesmen. There were, for example, no trade
       labourers among the late entrants to council
       employment.

(3)   The diminished prospect for 'steady' employ-
       ment was the main reason cited for some 30
       painters leaving the Department in the year
       up to September 1977 (Press and Journal, 8
       September 1977).

6 The threshold of retirement

LATE WORKING LIVES

The foregoing data suggest the existence of widely
different late working lives among male manual
workers. Continued employment in the face of
organisational change, skill redundancy, industrial
senescence or impaired health depended on two
organisational features. The ability of an
employing organisation to provide light or alternative work opportunities depends on the organisation's technical division of labour. The number
and range of jobs in a particular employment
context is, quite obviously, a key factor in the
possibility of continued employment. Analytically
distinct from this, though, is managerial willingness to deploy older rather than any other category
of worker to the posts that are available. On
these two dimensions, Stoneywood Mill and the
Building and Works Department were quite
different.

   Stoneywood Mill had, in the past, been characterised by a wide range of manual jobs distinguished
by function and a variety of skill gradings. The
complex occupational structure of the mill had
traditionally included a number of lighter or less

demanding posts. Given the paternalistic background
of the mill, and the high value placed on long and
loyal service, older workers displaced by changed
organisational requirements, or by some measure of
incapacity, could be found alternative work. The
balance of redeployment opportunity and managerial
willingness to redeploy older workers was, however,
changing.

   The paper industry had been under pressure
throughout the 1970s and early 1980s from foreign
competition and increasing production costs.
Surviving firms were characterised by an increasingly specialised product manufactured by processes
that were technologically advanced to the point
where overall labour requirements were reduced, and
the traditional skills of the workforce altered.
Process innovation and product market changes had
the combined effect of transforming the workplace.
Mill management's ability to deploy older workers
to appropriate posts diminished, and their
traditional attempts to provide employment for
older workers to the state pensionable age were
replaced by an increased tendency to discharge
their paternalistic role by offering early retirement to older employees instead of declaring
redundancies. As a result, late working life
experiences of current workers were somewhat
different from those of retirees.

   The work histories of retired and current workers
revealed a marked incidence of internal job changing
in late working life. The overall level of job
changing had been higher for retirees, and the job
changes reported had been qualitatively different.
Among current workers, the changes were less likely
to be of a retrogressive nature. Jobs were changed
for ones having largely similar characteristics,
but this had not been the case for retired men.
Job changers in the latter group were much more
likely to have entered retirement from 'light work'
jobs than seems feasible for the current generation
of older workers. Truncated extension careers,
rather than transition careers, would appear to be
one of the products of the mill's changing market
and technological environment.

   In contrast to Stoneywood Mill, the Building and
Works Department had a division of labour based on
distinct trade groupings, and a traditionally

unbridgeable gulf between skilled and unskilled
jobs. Other than a limited number of depot jobs,
there were few light work opportunities. However,
in a building industry context, most jobs in the
department could be regarded as 'lighter' because
they were, in Aberdeen, of the repair and maintenance variety. Typically, these men had spent their
earlier years in the more rigorous setting of private sector construction work where job security was
minimal, and health and strength vital for continued
participation. The jobs offered by the department
were not, however, in comparison with many manual
jobs, light and easy in nature. Awkward and heavy
tasks were involved, and many trades had to contend
with working out in wet and cold conditions.
Industrial senescence or health impairment were not
easily accommodated with the redeployment of men to
less-demanding work. When an older worker's
performance became problematic, it could only be
handled by trade foremen's discretionary redeployment to easier tasks within the normal range of
work. If this did not happen, or proved an
inadequate solution to the problem, early retirement
was the only option as depot jobs were an extremely
scarce resource.

Change came to the department in the form of a
legislative framework demanding a closer approximation to private sector business practice. The
demand for notional competitiveness found
expression, at worker level, in the closer monitoring of work, and the tighter association of pay
and performance. Any 'slowing up' by older
workers would soon become obvious in the performance monitoring arrangements, and inquiries would
be made. This, allied to administrative restructuring which replaced trade foremen with multi-trade
supervisors, changed the tenor of late working
life. Informal redeployment within the normal
workload became more difficult, and performance
monitoring meant that the older worker's control
over pacing was much reduced.

Among the department's retirees, only 41.7 per
cent, in total, had experienced late working life
job changes. This figure was, furthermore,
distorted by the level of late entry, i.e. men
joining the department at 54 years or older. Of
all retired men, only 25 per cent had experienced
job changes within the department. As Table 6.1

shows, these figures are in marked contrast to the mill where 58.5 per cent, in total, of the retirees had had at least one job change, and 87.5 per cent of that job changing had taken place within the mill.

Table 6.1

Retired men: comparison of job changing patterns

	Stoneywood Mill	Building and Works Department
	Per cent	Per cent
Total job changing between age 54 years, and retirement. (Internal redeployment plus late entry)	58.5	41.7
Job changing arising from internal redeployment	51.2	25.0
Internal redeployment as a percentage of total job changes	87.5	60.0

Table 6.2

Retired men: aspects of light work gained in last or only internal job change

	Stoneywood Mill		Building and Works Department		Both Organisations	
	No.	Per cent	No.	Per cent	No.	Per cent
Three or more aspects of light work gained	14	66.7	2	22.2	16	53.3
Fewer or no aspects of light work gained or reversal involved	7	33.3	7	77.8	14	46.7
Totals	21	100.0	9	100.0	30	100.0

(p = 0.032, significant at 0.05 level)

It is not just that internal redeployment was a much rarer phenomenon at the Building and Works Department, there was a noticeable difference in the extent to which changes produced lighter work. As Table 6.2 shows, two-thirds of the mill retirees had experienced alteration to three or more job elements on internal redeployment, but this was the case for less than a quarter of the council retirees who had changed jobs within the department.

While it must be borne in mind that they had incomplete work histories, it would appear that the current generation of older workers were finding a much changed situation. As shown in Table 6.3, the Stoneywood workers still demonstrated a fairly high level of job changing as one might expect with extensive process innovation; but the changes were of a decidedly less retrogressive nature than had been reported by retirees. Older employees at the Building and Works Department had a much lower incidence of internal job changing in late working life with very little indication of retrogression.

Table 6.3

Current workers: internal job changing and, where appropriate, aspects of light work gained as a result of last internal job change

	Stoneywood Mill		Building and Works Department		Both Organis- ations	
	No.	Per cent	No.	Per cent	No.	Per cent
INTERNAL JOB CHANGERS						
Three or more aspects of light work gained	2	11.8	1	6.3	3	9.1
Fewer or no aspects of light work gained or reversal involved	6	35.3	2	12.5	8	24.2
NON-CHANGERS	9	52.9	13	81.3	22	66.7
Totals	17	100.0	16	100.1	33	100.0

The organisational context of late working life
has a bearing on the way that older workers view
themselves and their chances of continued employment. At the Building and Works Department, where
skill and experience were not invalidated by process
innovation, and age did not present the same level
of employment vulnerability, current workers were
more optimistic about their chances of continuing in
their jobs to the state pensionable age than were
their counterparts at Stoneywood Mill. Equally, as
Tables 6.4 and 6.5 show, older employees at the
Building and Works Department were less likely to
think of themselves as being in a different
category to other workers; and more likely to deny
the proposition that a man's work deteriorates with
age.

Table 6.4

Current workers: extent to which they thought of
themselves as being in a different category to
other workers

	Stoneywood Mill		Building and Works Department		Both Organis- ations	
	No.	Per cent	No.	Per cent	No.	Per cent
Considered themselves in a different category	8	53.3	1	6.3	9	29.0
Did not consider themselves to be in a different category	7	46.7	15	93.8	22	71.0
Totals	15(*)	100.0	16	100.1	31	100.0

(*) Two ambivalent responses excluded

(p = 0.0054, significant at 0.01 level)

Table 6.5

Current workers: reactions to the idea that a man's work deteriorates with age

	Stoneywood Mill		Building and Works Department		Both Organisations	
	No.	Per cent	No.	Per cent	No.	Per cent
Agreement	14	82.4	7	43.8	21	63.6
Rejection	3	17.7	9	56.3	11	33.3
Totals	17	100.1	16	100.1	33	99.9

(p = 0.0474, significant at 0.05 level)

Organisational circumstances are not only related to how older workers feel about themselves as workers, but also to their ability to exert some control over the timing of their retirement.

These circumstances determine the point of entry into retirement except in those cases where a major health problem, or injury, causes total work incapacity. Employing organisations differ in the routine performance demands placed on older manual workers. They also differ in their capacity and willingness to redeploy, into more manageable jobs, those who are industrially senescent or who have some degree of health impairment. Changes in organisational capacity, and managerial willingness to redeploy, resulting from changes in the labour market for specific skills, process innovation, and alterations to the product market or legislative framework in which the organisation operates, not only modify the character of late working life, but determine its length.

Control over the timing of retirement is, at best, incomplete but labour market position and labour market history have an influence on the degree of control possible for the older worker. Even if older workers are fit and healthy, whether they can remain in employment to the state pensionable age is determined by organisational circumstances. This vulnerability is amplified when the

factors of poor health or industrial senescence are
added.

The present study suggests that industrial
senescence and health impairment were more likely
to result in early retirement at the Building and
Works Department than they were at Stoneywood Mill,
although changed circumstances in the latter meant
that less protection was now afforded such older
workers. On the other hand, control over retirement timing was greater for fit and healthy council
employees because there was a strong demand for
their skills. The ability of such workers to
decide on the appropriate time for retirement was,
however, limited by the maximum retirement age
policy and the fact that relatively few of the men
interviewed had at least 25 years service by the
time they reached 60 years, when they could have
opted for early retirement with normal benefits.
At Stoneywood Mill, control over the timing of
retirement had diminished even for fit older men
because, with changed product markets and process
innovation, the demand for their skills and
experience had weakened. Like older men in other
industrial settings, their hold on a niche in the
labour market was increasingly tenuous.

FEELINGS ABOUT RETIREMENT

The significance of pre-retirement occupation, per
se, for feelings about retirement is not denied in
the literature, indeed it underpins, implicitly,
much of the comparative research, and finds
clearest expression in the work of Friedmann and
Havighurst (1977). However, the work of Thomae,
and Lehr and Dreher reported in Havighurst et al
(1969) has indicated that organisational circumstances provide another dimension for comparative
research. Moreover, organisational differences can
transcend the similarity in experiences provided
by shared occupation. These insights do not,
however, extend to a consideration of the relationship between late working life experiences in a
particular organisation and feelings about retirement from that organisation. Their contribution
centres on the broader perspective of organisations
as distinct historical products with differing
'social climates'.

The present study has sought to utilise these
insights on broad historical differences, and
extend the analysis with consideration of late working life circumstances. The data suggest that the
organisational context of late working life has a
bearing on feelings about retirement.

(a) Retirees

Table 6.6

Retired men: reported feelings about
retirement at the point of retiral

	Stoneywood Mill		Building and Works Department		Both Organis- ations	
	No.	Per cent	No.	Per cent	No.	Per cent
Favourable	14	34.2	22	61.1	36	46.8
Unfavourable	27	65.9	14	38.9	41	53.3
Totals	41	100.1	36	100.0	77	100.1

(X^2 = 4.63, Yates' Correction applied, 1 deg. f.,
significant at 0.05 level)

Overall, 34.2 per cent of mill retirees reported
that they had wanted to retire as against 65.9 per
cent who would have preferred to carry on working.
At one extreme, there were those who had been
anxious to start their retirement; but usually
retirees spoke of their unwillingness to give up
work, and some even acknowledged that they had
dreaded retirement. Building and Works retirees,
on the other hand, were more likely to report that
they had been favourably inclined to retirement.
It is suggested here that the explanation for the
different response patterns is to be found in the
circumstances of late working life. First, though,
it would be useful to consider the data on feelings
about retirement from age and health retirees which
were masked in Table 6.6.

Table 6.7 shows that for men who retired at the
state pensionable age, the patterns of positive and
negative feelings about retirement were directionally congruent with those for all retirees, but

varied in amplitude. In comparison with the data of
Table 6.6, it can be seen that age retirees from
the mill were marginally less likely to be unfavourably disposed to retirement and council age retirees
were noticeably more likely to report a favourable
disposition than were retirees as a whole.
Retiring at the state pensionable age would seen
to increase the likelihood of positive feelings
about retirement, but this is far outweighed by
organisational disparities that were still very much
in evidence.

Table 6.7

Retired men: reported feelings about retirement by
those who retired at 65 years

	Stoneywood Mill		Building and Works Department		Both Organis- ations	
	No.	Per cent	No.	Per cent	No.	Per cent
Favourable	9	45.0	10	83.3	19	59.4
Unfavourable	11	55.0	2	16.7	13	40.6
Totals	20	100.0	12	100.0	32	100.0

(p = 0.036, significant at 0.05 level)

Those who retired at 65 years from the mill, or
the council, tended to come by very different routes
to their retirement. At Stoneywood Mill, the high
incidence of retrogressive job changing had served
to protect older workers from the more extreme
elements of manual work. The paternalistic
protection of older men had masked their diminished
work abilities and had, on balance, given them
reason to express reluctance about leaving jobs
that were manageable - even at 65 years.

It's a hell of a feeling when you come
away from the mill, and you say, 'That's
it,'and you come home and say, 'What
happens now?' Wait for the crematorium
or something like that. That's the
worst bit, I think, coming home after
doing all that time in the mill, you
know, and you sit here and look at the

wife and say, 'What's going to happen
now?' People think it's money and
leisure, and cruises and stuff like
that. It's just out!
(Retired mill employee)

I asked them if I could ... [stay
on past 65 years] ... I asked Mr. (Y),
and he said, 'Well, if it was in my
power to do so I wouldn't let you go
out those doors. I'd keep you back.'
I said, 'You know I don't want to
retire,' and he said, 'Well, I'm
sorry, but you'll have to.' There
was no way of being kept on ... just
had to go and make way for somebody
else.
(Retired mill employee)

Those who retired at 65 years from the Building and
Works Department, on the other hand, were largely in
favour of retirement because it was reached,
typically, without a reduction in the demands placed
on them. Equally, performance monitoring added a
stressful note to their everyday work. In these
circumstances, retirement was usually welcomed as a
respite from the rigours of the job.

If it had been possible, would you have
stayed on?

No, not in that job. I was desperately
tired, that's what I'm saying.
(Retired council employee)

As I said, plastering was a heavy job ...
As you get older your muscles are just
not the same. I was fine, but when I
was polishing a ceiling ... what we call
polishing a ceiling, a last rub, you
know ... It's hard. You put a smoothness
on to it. I'd get, maybe, less than
half-an-hour on the ceiling and I was
dead, you know. You get that as you
get older. But then you get fellows in
jobs that they can stick at till they're
eighty ... If I'd have been in an
office job, I'd have never dreamed of
retiring; but a heavy job, like the
building trade ... you're sort of -
well, I was - glad to get away from it,

you know. You began to feel your aches
and pains when you came home.
(Retired council employee)

It was really getting too hard for you.
If I'd have got a lighter job, I might
have done. I don't think I could have
stood it after sixty-five, like, because
as I said, the winters were terrible.
(Retired council employee)

Working at the Building and Works Department,
while it might have been physically easier - because
of its repair and maintenance character - than many
private sector jobs, was not easy in comparison with
most types of work. As the men had moved into late
working life, they had often found themselves in
some physical stress even if they were not actually
in poor health. Building trade work required
considerable bodily exertion - climbing, working with
arms above head height, twisting into confined
spaces, lifting and pushing. Even if there were no
specific health problems, ageing brought the
increasing probability of a mismatch between the
physical demands of the job and the individual's
capacity to meet them. Through late working life,
employees were getting to the point where they
wanted a reduction in work demands. However,
there were very few light work opportunities within
the normal range of trade activities, and even
those men who had transition late working life
careers did not, typically, experience the same
degree of retrogression as had been possible at
Stoneywood Mill.

The proportion of health retirees was quite
similar in the two groups of retired men. They
constituted 39 per cent of the mill group, and 42
per cent of council retirees. Their feelings about
retirement had, however, been quite different.

Health retirees from Stoneywood were more likely
to view their retirement unfavourably than mill
retirees generally, and were quite different from
Building and Works health retirees who, by a small
margin, had favoured retirement.

Table 6.8

Retired men: reported feelings about retirement by those who retired for health reasons

	Stoneywood Mill		Building and Works Department		Both Organis- ations	
	No.	Per cent	No.	Per cent	No.	Per cent
Favourable	2	12.5	8	53.3	10	32.3
Unfavourable	14	82.5	7	46.7	21	67.7
Totals	16	100.0	15	100.0	31	100.0

($p = 0.0193$, significant at the 0.025 level)

Stoneywood health retirees were in a situation that enhanced a sense of relative deprivation when poor health precipitated their retirement. As the mill had a tradition of redeploying older men into lighter work when their health failed, the feeling that retirement really was the 'end of the line' was all the more apparent.

I dreaded the day when I would have to pack up. I knew it was coming, for a long time. I knew it was coming ...

Why do you say dreaded?

... financially ... and because I knew once that day came I was on the scrap heap.

You really feel that?

Oh yes. I mean if I couldn't work for Wiggins Teape who was I going to work for ... I feared the abrupt end, and that was it. I was told by my doctor to go down and tell them that I wouldn't be back to work. That's a shakeup, and I was just sixty then. (Retired mill employee)

At the Building and Works Department, with its much weaker pattern of retrogressive job changing even for those with impaired health, health retire- ment was viewed more in relation to the impossibility of maintaining performance within the normal range of tasks.

> We used to take out the window, and take
> them downstairs and outside; and kneel
> down, you know. Well, it was maybe dry,
> but the warmth here ... [indicates knees]
> ... it used to draw up the damp from
> under the ground, and that's why I got
> arthritis in the knees, you know ...
> It was this outside work I was doing -
> and the climbing and things like that -
> so I took the year early.
> (Retired council employee)

Furthermore, retiring from the mill in poor health
was, if we assume an association between length of
service and a sense of loss on termination of that
service, a much bigger wrench for mill health
retirees than was the case for their Building and
Works counterparts. The mean average service for
the mill's health retirees was 36.6 years, as
opposed to 18.0 years at the Building and Works
Department. Length of service had an important
symbolic value to men at the mill, and it was not
unknown for health retirees to comment adversely on
their condition for what it had done to their
service record as much as for its impact on other
aspects of their lives.

> The wife'll tell you, I took a long,
> long time to make up my mind. I was
> wanting to do my 50 years service,
> but I took another turn. It wasn't
> a heart attack, it was bleeding at
> the throat. Well, I took it to be
> the throat, I didn't really know
> what it was ... They found it was a
> hiatus hernia. I was always wary of
> myself after that ... It really made
> me think then. I was wondering before
> this came up what would happen if I
> did take early retirement ...
>
> WIFE ... but he's stubborn, you see ...
>
> ... but I didn't want it through that.
> I was determined to try for my 50
> years ... but, it so happened that it
> wasn't to be, and as the foreman said,
> 'You'd just as well be at home, you're
> not losing anything.'
> (Retired mill employee)

At first sight, it could be argued that the
present study adds little to the Lehr and Dreher
(in Havighurst et al, 1969) findings about organisational differences in the pattern of retirement
attitudes because occupation was not held constant.
However, even allowing for this limitation, it
would seem safe to conclude - given the data on age
and health retirees - that the way older men feel
about retirement is influenced by the organisational
context of late working life. In particular, the
availability of lighter, less-demanding work and a
managerial willingness to redeploy older workers,
would appear salient to the formation of retirement
attitudes. This conclusion is congruent with the
more general summary statement of Lehr and Dreher,
and the strain-specific observation by Jacobson
(1972a).

> The most positive attitude toward
> retirement correlated best with the
> most negative perception of the
> immediate work situation.
> (Lehr and Dreher in Havighurst
> et al, 1969, p. 127)

> The majority of those employed in
> 'heavy' and 'moderate' jobs, 65.9
> per cent and 60.8 per cent respectively,
> would have chosen to retire below the
> age of 65 had the decision rested
> entirely with them. This attitude was
> held by only a quarter of the men in
> 'light' jobs.
> (Jacobson, 1972a, p. 197)

Read in conjunction with Jacobson and Lehr and
Dreher, the present study suggests grounds to
question assumptions about occupation, per se, as
the main variable for comparative retirement
research. People retire from specific jobs rather
than from occupations. What they think about
retirement is rooted in the late working life
context of occupational practice. Further support
for this contention comes from a review of current
workers' feelings about early retirement.

(b) Current workers

Table 6.9

Current workers: feelings about early retirement

	Stoneywood Mill		Building and Works Department		Both Organis- ations	
	No.	Per cent	No.	Per cent	No.	Per cent
Favourable	11	64.7	9	56.3	20	60.6
Ambivalent	3	17.7	5	31.3	8	24.2
Unfavourable	3	17.7	2	12.5	5	15.2
Totals	17	100.1	16	100.1	33	100.0

When we turn to consider current older workers at
the mill, we find that they were more favourably
inclined to early retirement than retirees had been
to their retirement. The circumstances of this
cohort of ageing workers had changed; proceeding
further along the path of process innovation,
demanning and the development of mechanisms for
early withdrawal from the labour force. As Table
6.9 shows, over 64 per cent were positively
inclined, not only to retirement, but to early
retirement.

   A few men were better described as ambivalent
about the idea of early retirement, rather than
unfavourably inclined. In all cases, this ambivalence was the result of an incomplete picture of the
financial arrangements. A great deal of confusion
surrounded the types of early retirement possible,
and detailed financial advice was said to be
elusive.

   I mean, you get bits of information from
   other people that are retiring, you know.
   Now, one chap, he retired ... a year
   older than me, doing exactly the same
   job. He's retired. He took a lump sum
   from them, and didn't take any pension
   as far as I know. You don't pry too
   deeply into other people's affairs but
   you're always trying to pry to get a

171

lead for yourself. But that's what I
believe he did, or he took a lump sum,
and lowered his´pension so low that
it didn't count, you know. He got the
information because he did ... he went
up and, I believe, he created merry
hell with them to ... and they gave
him the facts, you know. But why can't
they do that before, and without you
having to go down on your bended knees,
and saying something like, you know,
'Give us some information.'
(Mill worker, aged 61 years)

   Relatively few of the current older workers said
that they would not consider early retirement.
Even allowing for the fact that these were 'prospective' statements rather than the 'retrospective'
accounts of retirees, there would appear to be a
larger proportion favourably inclined to retirement. For many, their continued participation in
the workforce was more as a result of the unsatis-
factory negotiation of conditions for withdrawal,
than a dogged desire to carry on to their 65th
birthday.

   These older men were increasingly beset by the
question of diminished utility, a situation that
fostered an enhanced consciousness of age (see
Table 6.4), and decline (see Table 6.5). Any
problems developing in their final years of mill
employment were unlikely to be resolved by transition careers; any job changing that did take place
was less likely (see Table 6.3) to produce a
lessening of work demands. In these circumstances,
early retirement was, at least, something worthy
of serious consideration.

   The contrast between mill retirees and current
older workers was quite marked. It was, of course,
possible that the retrospective accounts of
retirees gave undue emphasis to negative feelings
at retirement in accordance, loosely, with Kahn's
(1973) perceptive comments about the 'watery eye of
memory' (1). There is, perhaps, no way of being
absolutely certain that such a phenomenon did not
have a bearing on the retirees' accounts. However,
as outlined in the Appendix, an attempt was made
to minimise distorted recall. It might also be
argued that as the current older workers age they

172

will change their attitudes to retirement, echoing
the pattern reported by Lehr and Dreher (in
Havighurst et al, 1969). However, while men who
eventually have to retire early because of poor
health might come to disfavour retirement because
of the actual circumstances under which they have
to leave work, it is unlikely that a similar change
in feelings about retirement will occur for those
who do not leave on health grounds. Lehr and
Dreher's contrast of the retirement attitudes of
workers in the early stages of late working life,
and those of workers nearing the 'retirement age'
encapsulated a time-span much greater than that
which could apply at Stoneywood Mill. Lehr and
Dreher compared the attitudes of 50-55 year old,
and 60-65 year old workers. Current workers at
Stoneywood were no younger than 54 years at the time
of interview; their mean average age was 59.1
years, and 47.1 per cent were in their sixties.
In short, given age-related demanning, and their
awareness of it, their feelings about retirement
cannot be judged to have the same degree of detachment from the imminent possibility of retirement
that Lehr and Dreher's 50-55 year olds presumably
felt.

   The response profile for older employees at the
Building and Works Department was interesting in
that the proportion favourably inclined to early
retirement was very similar to that for retirees
in relation to their retirement. Given that the
slim possibility of light work had been made less
probable by recent organisational changes, one
might have expected to find more older workers
favourably inclined to early retirement. However,
two factors must be considered.

   First, at the Building and Works Department,
older employees' service levels were, relative to
their contemporaries at Stoneywood Mill, quite low.
At the Building and Works Department, current
workers had a mean average of 19.8 years service
at the time of interview in comparison with 28.1
years at the mill. Comparing the 2 groups of
current workers on the basis of 25 year service
levels (2), the differences were significant.

Table 6.10

Current workers: comparison of service levels at the time of interview

	Stoneywood Mill		Building and Works Department		Both Organis- ations	
	No.	Per cent	No.	Per cent	No.	Per cent
Less than 25 years service at the time of interview	6	35.3	13	81.3	19	57.6
25 years or longer service at the time of interview	11	64.7	3	18.8	14	42.4
Totals	17	100.0	16	100.1	33	100.0

(p = 0.009, significant at 0.01 level)

The relatively low levels of service at the department would, arguably, have served to limit the extent to which current workers indicated favourable disposition towards early retirement. Even if, in terms of stress occasioned by industrial senescence or the more competitive context of council employ-ment, they were not averse to retirement, the ability to finance early retirement was a separate matter. It is one thing to feel physically ready for retirement from that employment, and quite another to have the service necessary to 'trigger' immediate payment of the occupational pension.

Given the service histories of the current council employees, and the powerful inducements to carry on working as long as possible contained in the pension scheme, it was remarkable that so many of the current workers were favourably inclined to early retirement.

Second, as shown in Table 6.9, a number of current council employees expressed some ambivalence about early retirement. This ambivalence was grounded in the kind of pension problems outlined above. If this group had been characterised by longer

174

service, one might have expected the ambivalence to
resolve into a decidedly favourable perspective on
early retirement.

> Well, it all depends how things work out
> finance-wise, you see ... what they'd
> give us as a lump sum and as a weekly ...
> as opposed to working on, you see.
> (Council worker, aged 56 years)

> I'll miss my work. Oh aye. I mean, I'm
> still very active ... Although I say
> I'll miss it, I would have had no
> hesitation in taking early retirement
> if they'd have given me the full pension.
> I'd have retired to give a young person
> a job because I think this is a disaster
> in this country; young people not
> getting jobs and they're getting into
> mischief. There's no doubt about it.
> (Council worker, aged 63 years)

There was certainly reason to believe that, among
current workers, early retirement was a serious
consideration even if circumstances did not necess-
itate, or permit, the immediate translation of
thought into action.

> Since I left there's been a lot have
> taken early retirement to get away
> from the place. I know a few of them
> absolutely fed up, and a lot more
> would go ... as a matter of fact, the
> man that was foreman ... I just see
> him now and again, said, 'I'm dying to
> be sixty so I can get away.'
> (Retired council employee)

What about early retirement?

> I don't think so, no. Actually, it
> works both ways ... I said to the wife,
> 'There's a lot of the lads taking
> early retirement under the Government
> thing.' ... and she said, 'You're not
> thinking of taking that are you?' I
> said, 'I'm only saying that there's a
> few been doing it, you know. I was
> only saying what some were doing. I'm
> not saying that I would do it.' I'm
> not saying that I'm being swayed by my
> wife. I've got a mind of my own.

Actually, right now, I think I'm one of
the few that's going right on to the end.
There's that many taking early retirements,
and through ill-health. Quite a lot of
the boys have had to go through ill-
health, which is no fault of their's, of
course. That could happen to me; it
could happen to anybody, but other than
that ... As I say, I don't feel right
now that ... I'm not straining, you know
what I mean, with the job. I can climb
up a ladder, no bother; heights have
never bothered me, and still don't. I
don't see why you should if you're quite
enjoying your job, and you feel yourself
up to it. The only thing is, the bonus
system has introduced a wee bit of pressure
that you could have done without, you know.
You've got to produce, and I'm afraid
that's a thing they don't give much
thought to as you're getting older. If
you're not ... say I had a couple of
weeks now and I was feeling under par
but I still went to my work, but I
wasn't producing the performance, you see.
Now, they wouldn't sit down and say,
'Ah well, of course he's coming up to ...'
They'd come down and find out why my
performance had dropped. So, the bonus
has given that latter consideration, you
know ... There's nobody worries me. I've
probably got to make an appointment to
see the supervisor. That is a good thing
in a way because he trusts me to carry on
with the job. He doesn't have to go and
look. There's no complaints coming in so,
if there's no complaints, he leaves me
severely alone, you know. That's fine;
but if I was finding it difficult to make
this performance that would be a different
story.
(Council worker, aged 64 years)

Summarising, it would appear that late working
life circumstances and, indeed, labour market
history have a bearing on feelings about retirement.
It can be argued that changing late working life
circumstances at Stoneywood Mill were influential
in creating the disparity between retirees'
feelings about retirement, and current workers'

feelings about early retirement. Age-related demanning, and the reduced likelihood of light work, had made current workers cautious about the prospect of working to the state pensionable age. Given, also, the relatively high service levels that would have meant reasonable occupational pensions, and a pension scheme that, in the context of demanning, put few obstacles in the path of early retirement applications (3), current employees approached the end of their working lives at the mill in a different frame of mind to that of the retirees. At the Building and Works Department, on the other hand, retirees' feelings about their retirement closely matched current workers' feelings about early retirement. Here, though, with relatively low service levels and, at the time of the inter- views, no reason for management to seek labour force reductions, there was a noticeable strand of ambivalence. Arguably, if service levels had been higher, there would have been a far greater incidence of favourable early retirement responses.

CONCLUDING OBSERVATION

The changing labour market for older workers is a major problem in British society though it is disguised, to a large extent, by the assumption that early retirement is a state desired for what retirement has to offer. In fact, early retirement is, for many, better understood as exclusion from a workforce or, indeed, from the labour market.

The present study has outlined two very different sets of conditions for late working life, and has shown the effects of organisational change. Although, by no stretch of the imagination, can this work be described as definitive, it has clearly underwritten the need to focus our under- standing of retirement on specific employment contexts. For too long, retirement has been seen only in relation to ageing and prior occupation when, usefully, it can be viewed in relation to employment, and types of labour market history.

Further research is needed on the operation of early retirement as a demanning strategy in different employment contexts, and the types of vulnerability experienced by older workers in the years leading to the state pensionable age. The

foregoing is but a contribution to our understanding
of retirement as a changing social phenomenon.

NOTES

(1)   Kahn (1973, p. 29) makes the observation
       that memories are kinder in direct proportion
       to their length. Although he was referring
       to memories of performance, the point can be
       taken to have relevance to retrospective
       accounts of all kinds.

(2)   There were two factors in the Local Govern-
       ment Superannuation Scheme regulations which
       encouraged men to stay on as long as they
       were able.

       (a)   A man could retire between the ages
             of 60 and 65 years, but unless he had
             25 years of reckonable service, the
             full benefits would not be paid
             immediately. Men without a health
             problem who chose to take early
             retirement, but without 25 years
             reckonable service, had two options:
             (i)   to take an immediate reduced
                    pension and a reduced cash
                    lump sum, or
             (ii)   to have the full benefits
                    deferred.
             Given that the state pension would
             not be payable until the man reached
             the age of 65, these regulations
             provided a considerable inducement to
             stay at work as long as possible. If
             the Local Authority actually wanted to
             shed labour, the regulations allowed
             the payment of immediate 'normal'
             benefits to anyone between the ages of
             50 and 65 if they had at least 5 years
             of reckonable service. In addition,
             the Local Authority could 'enhance'
             service thus making an early retirement
             offer more attractive.

       (b)   The pension lump sum for married men
             was calculated on a two-stage basis.
             Service up to 1 April 1972 was allowed
             at one-eightieth of the final pension-
             able pay multiplied by the years of
             reckonable service. Service after

1 April 1972 was allowed at three-
eightieths as a multiplier in the
same equation.
Together, these points provide a powerful
inducement to stay on at work for as long as
possible. Ill-health retirement works as a
more generous basis (Pensions Communications
Limited, 1979).
(3)   The Wiggins Teape pension scheme allowed early
retirement for those over 50, but required the
individual to obtain company and pension
scheme trustees' approval. In the context of
demanning, such approval would have been
forthcoming.

Appendix: a note on methods

SOURCES OF INFORMATION

(a)   Interviews with older workers and retirees

The ways in which older workers adjust to changing
physiological and organisational realities would have
been best monitored at close quarters, and as it
happened. The strategy most appropriate to such a
task is, arguably, where the researcher becomes a
constituent part of the respondents' social world.
So the promise of participant observation (Vidich,
1969) was not without appeal given the concerns of
the present study.

   However, there were a number of problems in the
adoption of such a strategy for the present
research. First, while there are a number of
permutations possible in the 'participant' and the
'observer' elements (Gold, 1969; Smith, H., 1975), it
would have been difficult to establish research
roles that were equally convincing to current
workers with the Building and Works Department and
Stoneywood Mill, and to the retired employees of
both establishments. Second, neither the
'participant-as-observer' role exemplified by
Roth's (1963) study, nor the 'observer-as-

participant' role adopted by Becker (1977, pp. 25 - 38) can be effectively utilised without a substantial investment of time and, in the case of current workers, organisational facilitation. Thirdly, retired workers no longer existed in an organisational setting nor did they - even those from the paper mill - have a sufficiently uniform life-style to readily suggest a role opportunity for the researcher.

How then was it possible to gather accounts of the meanings given to events in late working life? Even for current workers, allowing time to intervene between events and data collection invites the problem of reconstructions 'glossing' those situations (1). At another level, it even taxes the accuracy of respondents' memories. In the present study it was possible for men of 70 years to be talking about events and feelings of some 15 years ago; failure of memory and the danger of re-construction were, therefore, not inconsiderable problems.

However, the following points do provide a measure of confidence in the adoption of a strategy other than participant observation. First, most sociological research relies, to some extent, on retrospective description and analysis by the respondent. Very little, if any, research 'transmits' the story as it is being unfurled and while participant observation offers something of a solution to this problem, it does not entirely avoid it. Second, even accounts gathered in very close temporal proximity to events are subject to the problem of rationalisation. After all, impression management is not solely a function of time. Accounts of what happened yesterday, or an hour ago, may be distorted by selective recall so, while time-lapse presents additional problems, it does not present unique problems (Musto and Benison, 1969).

Beyond these considerations, memory undoubtedly presents difficulties for research. There were, however, points that could be built into the research strategy. It appeared that events that respondents were personally involved in seemed to be better available for accurate recall (Bulmer, 1978). Further, Becker (1977, pp. 25 - 38) had argued the value of centralising the respondent's attention on their own experiences, so creating a

focus for the account. Generalisations made by the
respondent, he observed, could be usefully turned
back into specifics with a mixture of requests for
further information and scepticism (2).

With these points in mind, then, it was decided
that a strategy involving interviews with current
workers and retired men focussing on actual job
changes (3), and job content, would be adopted.
With this kind of focus it seemed that the meanings
attached to events would, within the limits already
discussed, be more reliably forthcoming. Equally,
it was thought that a sequential pattern to the
questions, reviewing occupational history in the
order that it happened, would provide additional
focussing for respondents.

To systematically gather a considerable amount of
factual information with explanations of how they
felt at certain points in late working life meant
that there was some value seen in both structured
and unstructured interview formats. Structured
interviews standardise the questions and, hence, the
form of the information received from respondents.
Although, for some purposes, they are an effective
research instrument, they are not without their
attendant problems (Denzin, 1970). One such problem
is manifest when the researcher feels that the
establishment of what amounts to a map of the
respondents' world - the significant events,
meanings, and actions - would be unjustified at the
outset. There were feelings of this kind with the
present study, and so a variation of the standardised, or structured interview format was used.
Certain features of late working life were to be
included - job changes, job content, feelings about
work and the prospect of retirement. Such features
could be appropriately standardised. However, it
was recognised that respondents had inhabited
occupational environments of which outsiders would
have little knowledge, and experiences which could
not be totally known in advance of the research.

The format adopted approximated to a 'focussed'
or 'non-schedule standardised' interview (Denzin,
1970), i.e. the minimal scope of the interview
was pre-determined, but the sequence was varied
according to the respondent's perceptions of
salience. Interview schedules were used, therefore,
but it was thought necessary to allow respondents

to answer in a way that best suited their re-
collections and, of equal importance, to amplify
their answers by reference to the circumstances
forming a background to specific events and their
feelings. While attempting to standardise the
information collected, it would have violated the
purpose of the interview if digression and
alternative perspectives had not been afforded their
true significance(4).

Acknowledging not only the likelihood, but also
the value, of material offered to supplement the
areas covered by the questionnaire posed a recording
problem. To make sure that this kind of data was
not 'lost' to the final report, the interviews were
taped. All the interviews were conducted in the
homes of respondents and ranged in length from
about 45 minutes to 2 hours with, perhaps, 1 hour
being a fair guide to the average duration.

(b) Other sources

Background information on the two employing organisations was available from a variety of sources.
The Building and Works Department was more access-
ible in terms of publically available material
with, for example, the minutes of the Works
Committee and the annual report of the Building and
Works Department being subject to statutory
provisions for information disclosure. The paper
mill was well-documented historically, and it was
possible to obtain adequate background to current
problems from trade journals. Newspaper accounts
held in the Local Studies Library at Aberdeen and
the clippings archive at Aberdeen Journals Ltd.,
were used with the usual caution (5) but proved
to be of value in considering the public dimensions of organisational problems.

The problems facing the Building and Works
Department were a matter of current debate and
visits to two conferences organised by the Institute
of Management Services (6) were useful in developing an understanding of the national context of
problems. Additionally, telephone conversations
with, and printed information from, the pressure
group ADLO - the Association of Direct Labour
Organisations - were valuable.

Finally, interviews with management employees in

Stoneywood Mill, and both Manpower Services and the
Building and Works Department at the City of
Aberdeen District Council were important for
clarification of the complex problems that confronted management in the two organisations.

STATISTICAL ANALYSIS

Small samples limit the confidence one can place in
generalisation, and throughout the present study
there was an awareness that more organisational
examples and, perforce, greater respondent numbers
would have enhanced the utility of the work.
However, this study was of an exploratory nature
and, as such, faced the problem of having a relatively broad scope in relation to the sample numbers
that were manageable (7). It was felt that this
problematic combination of scope and sample size,
although an ultimate limitation of the study, was
not in itself sufficient reason to postpone
exploration of the issues identified in Chapter 1.

   Although there were 110 respondents, a research
design that focussed on two organisations and two
respondent statuses, worker and retirees, inevit-
ably faced problems of numerical adequacy with
cross-tabulations. This presented particular
difficulties for the calculation of statistical
significance.

   Where numbers permit, i.e. when $n \geqslant 20$, and where
expected values are $\geqslant 5$, X^2 has been used to
indicate the level of significance. For 2 x 2
contingency tables satisfying these conditions,
Yates' Correction was applied to provide a more
realistic approximation of significance levels
(Anderson and Zelditch, 1968). In 2 x 2 tables
where $n < 20$ and expected values were less than 5,
exact levels of significance were found using
Finney et al (1963), a tabulation of Fisher's
Exact Test calculations for a range of 2 x 2
contingency tables.

NOTES

(1)   Terkel (1970) circumvents this problem by
      regarding the methodological difficulty as
      the precision of factual recall. However,

his recognition of the 'invisible scar' would suggest that the difficulties are, in reality, more profound.

(2) In the present study, my lack of first-hand knowledge of the work settings and the age-difference between myself and the respondents facilitated exploitation of this insight.

(3) Roth (1963) suggests that such nodal points in career timetables have a particular importance for individuals. Hence, their role as 'triggers' in the current study.

(4) Trevor Lummis has argued (see discussion reports in Oral History, Vol. 1, No. 4, 1971) that there is an additional advantage in the mixed model of questionnaire and tape. The questionnaire can have a verification role in relation to data collected using 'the conversational approach'.

(5) Thompson (1971) notes that historians who would recognise the limitations of present-day newspapers often appear to 'suspend their disbelief' when it comes to old newspapers.

(6) The two conferences, both entitled 'Direct Labour Organisations - Two Years On' were held in Stafford (15 June 1983), and in Glasgow (22 February 1984). The second was a Scottish edition of the first, with similar themes, but geared to the fact that the legislation is effectively 'behind' that applying in England and Wales. The difference is one of timing rather than substance.

(7) For an account of a similar problem, see the points made by Salaman (1971b) in relation to an earlier statement of hypotheses (Salaman, 1971a).

Bibliography

Abercrombie, N. and Hill, S., Paternalism and
  patronage, British Journal of Sociology, vol. 27,
  no. 4, December 1976.
Aberdeen Daily Journal, Stoneywood paper works;
  remarkable progress of an important industry,
  23 August 1901.
Aberdeen Daily Journal, Late Mr. Francis Pirie: a
  personal appreciation, 15 May 1915.
Aberdeen Daily Journal, Stoneywood's 150th. anniver-
  sary: works celebration today, 14 August 1920.
ADLO News, Issue no. 1, Association of Direct
  Labour Organisations, September 1982.
ADLO News, Issue no. 3, Association of Direct
  Labour Organisations, November 1983.
Alexander, A., The politics of local government in
  the United Kingdom, Longman, London, 1982.
Anderson, T. and Zelditch, M., A basic course in
  statistics with sociological applications, Holt,
  Rinehart, Winston, New York, 1968 edition.
Atchley, R., The sociology of retirement, Schenkman,
  New York, 1976.
Atkinson, J., Manpower strategies for flexible
  organisations, Personnel Management, vol. 16, no.
  8, August 1984.
Bartlett, J., Alexander Pirie and Sons of Aberdeen
  1860-1914, Business History, January 1980.

Becker, H., Sociological work, Transaction, New Brunswick, 1977 edition.
Belbin, R., Older people and heavy work, British Journal of Industrial Medicine, vol. 12, 1955.
Bendix, R., Work and authority in industry, Harper and Row, 1963 edition.
Beynon, H. and Blackburn, R., Perceptions of work: variations within a factory, Cambridge University Press, Cambridge, 1972.
Blau, P., The dynamics of bureaucracy: a study of interpersonal relations in two government agencies, University of Chicago Press, London, 1973 edition.
Braverman, H., Labour and monopoly capital, Monthly Review Press, New York, 1974.
British Institute of Management, Redundancy policies - a study of current practice in 350 companies (1974), cited in Department of Employment Gazette, p. 1033, September 1978.
Bromley, D., The psychology of human ageing, Penguin, Harmondsworth, 1974.
Brown, R., Age and paced work, Occupational Psychology, vol. 31, 1957.
Buckley, K., Trade unionism in Aberdeen 1878-1900, Oliver and Boyd, Edinburgh, 1955.
Bulmer, M., (ed) Mining and social change, Croom Helm, London, 1978.
Casey, B. and Bruche, G., Work or retirement?, Gower, Aldershot, 1983.
City of Aberdeen District Council, City of Aberdeen: Department of Building and Works annual report and accounts for the year ended 31 March 1983, September 1983.
City of Aberdeen District Council, Department of Building and Works: annual report and accounts for the year ended 31 March 1984, August 1984.
City of Aberdeen District Council, Department of Building and Works: annual report and accounts for the year ended 31 March 1985, September 1985.
Clark, F. le gros, The working fitness of older men: a study of men over 60 in the building industry, Nuffield Foundation, London, 1954.
Clark, F. le gros, Bus workers in their later lives: a study of the employment of 300 drivers and conductors from the age of 60 onwards, Nuffield Foundation, London, 1957 (a).

Clark, F., le gros, Ageing on the factory floor: the production of domestic furniture: an inquiry made through works records and work descriptions into the prospects of ageing men within a mechanized industry, Nuffield Foundation, London, 1957 (b).

Clark, F. le gros, Workers nearing retirement: studies based upon interviews with older workers in the industrial town of Slough, Nuffield Foundation, London, 1963.

Clark, F. le gros, Work, age and leisure, Michael Joseph, London, 1966.

Clark, S.D., The employability of older workers: a review of research findings, Department of Labour, Ottawa, 1959, cited in Clark, F. le gros, (op.cit.), 1966.

Conrad, R., Comparison of paced and unpaced performance at a packing task, Occupational Psychology, vol. 29, 1955, cited in Brown, R., (op.cit.), 1957.

Crawford, M., Retirement and disengagement, Human Relations, vol. 24, no. 3, 1971.

Cruickshank, J., Newhills: the annals of the parish, Cruickshank, Aberdeen, 1934.

Cruickshank, J., Alexander Piries and Sons Ltd., paper manufacturers: Stoneywood and Waterton works 1770 - 1945, (typescript), 1946.

D'Amico, R. and Brown, T., Patterns of labour mobility in a dual economy: the case of semi-skilled and unskilled workers, Social Science Research, vol. 11, 1982.

Dennis, N., Henriques, F. and Slaughter, C., Coal is our life: an analysis of a Yorkshire mining community, Tavistock, London, 1969 edition.

Denselow, R., What will happen when the old outnumber the young?, The Listener, 8 December 1983.

Denzin, N., The research act in sociology: a theoretical introduction to sociological methods, Butterworths, London, 1970.

Department of Employment, Job Release Scheme for men aged 64 and women aged 59, Pamphlet PL 664, 1981.

Department of Employment, Job Release Scheme, Pamphlet PL 741, 1984.

Department of Employment Gazette, Age and redundancy, September 1978.

Department of the Environment, Local authority direct labour consultation paper, HMSO, London, 1979.

Department of the Environment/Audit Inspectorate,
  Direct labour organisations maintenance, HMSO,
  London, 1983.
Diack, W., History of the trades council and trade
  union movement in Aberdeen, Aberdeen Trades
  Council, Aberdeen, 1939.
Doering, M., Rhodes, S. and Schuster, M., The
  ageing worker: research and recommendations,
  Sage, Beverly Hills, 1983.
Dzierzek, A., The construction industry and work
  study, Work Study, April 1969.
Economist (The), The unsolved riddle of why people
  age, 10 January 1981.
Elliott, C., Age and internal labour mobility of
  semi-skilled workers, Occupational Psychology,
  vol. 40, 1966.
Employment Gazette, An increase in earlier retire-
  ment for men, April 1980.
Employment Gazette, Regional and age variations in
  unemployment flow, February 1984.
Evans, A., Measures to make the jobs go round,
  Personnel Management, January 1979.
Evening Express (Aberdeen), Decision on Council
  works put off, 16 November 1977.
Evening Express (Aberdeen), Church set to celebrate
  centenary, 1 September 1979.
Evening Express (Aberdeen), Painter shortage leaves
  city houses empty, 10 September 1980.
Evening Express (Aberdeen), Problem of tenants
  refusing homes, 21 October 1981.
Evening Express (Aberdeen), Penpushing bid to beat
  computer bug, 27 July 1983.
Finney, D. et al, Tables for testing significance in
  a 2x2 contingency table, Cambridge University
  Press, Cambridge, 1963.
Flynn, N., Direct labour organisations, Local
  Government Studies, March/April 1981.
Flynn, N. and Walsh, K., Managing direct labour
  organisations, Institute of Local Government
  Studies/University of Birmingham, Birmingham,
  1982.
Flynn, N., Walsh, K. and Halford, R., DLOs:
  coping with the profit targets, Local Government
  Chronicle, 19 August 1983.
Fraser, R., Work 2, Penguin, Harmondsworth, 1969.
Friedmann, E., Havighurst, R. et al, The meaning
  of work and retirement, Arno Press, New York,
  1977 edition.

Gallagher, B., Managing DLO operations, paper presented at Institute of Management Services conference, Glasgow, February 1984 (unpublished).

General Household Survey (1980), HMSO, London, 1982.

General Household Survey (1982), HMSO, London, 1984.

General Household Survey (1983), HMSO, London, 1985.

Glenn, N. and Weaver, C., Enjoyment of work by full-time workers in the U.S., 1955 and 1980, Public Opinion Quarterly, vol. 46, 1982.

Gold, R., Roles in sociological field observations, in McCall, C. and Simmons, J. (eds), Issues in participant observation: a text and reader, Addison-Wesley, Reading (Massachusetts), 1969.

Gouldner, A., Patterns of industrial bureaucracy, Free Press, New York, 1954.

Gouldner, A., Cosmopolitans and locals: toward an analysis of latent social roles, in Grusky, O. and Miller, G., The sociology of organizations, Free Press, New York, 1970.

Growing Older, Government White Paper, Cmnd. 8173, HMSO, London, 1981.

Guest, R., Work careers and aspirations of autom-obile workers, in Galenson, W. and Lipset, L., Labor and trade unionism: an interdisciplin-ary reader, John Wiley, New York, 1960.

Hall, K. and Miller, I., Retraining and tradition: the skilled worker in an era of change, George Allen and Unwin, London, 1975.

Havighurst, R. et al, Adjustment to retirement, van Gorcum, Assen, 1969.

Heron, A., Middle-aged and older people in industry, Works Management, December 1957.

Heron, A., Chown, S. et al, Ageing and the semi-skilled: a survey in manufacturing industry on Merseyside, Medical Research Council Memorandum no. 40, HMSO, London, 1961.

Hochschild, A., Disengagement theory: a critique and proposal, American Sociological Review, vol. 40, 1975.

Hughes, E., Dilemmas and contradictions of status, American Journal of Sociology, March 1945.

Hull, F. et al, The effect of technology on alienation from work, Work and Occupations, vol. 9, no. 1, February 1982.

Hunt, A., The elderly at home, OPCS/Social Survey Division, HMSO, London, 1978.

Hunter, L., Reid, G. and Boddy, D., Labour problems of technological change, George Allen and Unwin, London, 1970.

International Labour Office, *Introduction to work study*, ILO, Geneva, 1969 edition.

International Labour Organisation, *The age of retirement*, ILO, Geneva, 1954.

Jacobs, A., The chaos behind the giant Local Government Bill, *Local Government Chronicle*, 25 July 1980.

Jacobson, D., Fatigue-producing factors in industrial work and pre-retirement attitudes, *Occupational Psychology*, vol. 46, 1972 (a).

Jacobson, D., Willingness to retire in relation to job strain and type of work, *Industrial Gerontology*, vol. 13, 1972 (b).

Jahoda, M., *Employment and unemployment: a social psychological analysis*, Cambridge University Press, Cambridge, 1982.

Jolly, J., Creigh, S. and Mingay, A., *Age as a factor in employment*, Research Paper no. 11, Unit for Manpower Studies/Department of Employment, HMSO, London, April 1980.

Joyce, P., *Work, society and politics: the culture of the factory in later Victorian England*, Harvester Press, Brighton, 1980.

Kahn, R., *The boys of summer*, Signet, New York, 1973.

Kreckel, R., Unequal opportunity and labour market segmentation, *Sociology*, vol. 14, 1980.

Landes, D., The European experience of industrialisation, in Burns, T., *Industrial man*, Penguin, Harmondsworth, 1969.

Lane, T. and Roberts, K., *Strike at Pilkingtons*, Fontana, London, 1971.

Lehr, U. and Dreher, G., Determinants of attitudes towards retirement, in Havighurst, R. et al, *op. cit.*, 1969.

Litras, T., The battle over retirement policies and practices, *Personnel Journal*, February 1979.

Local Government (Direct Labour Organisations) (Competition) (Scotland) Regulations (The), SI 1984/159, HMSO, London, 1984.

Local Government, Planning and Land Act, HMSO, London, 1980.

Local Government (Scotland) Act, HMSO, London, 1973.

Lummis, T., The occupational community of East Anglian fishermen: an historical dimension through oral evidence, *British Journal of Sociology*, vol. 28, no. 1, March 1977.

Lyon, P., *Late working life and retirement: a sociological study of the retirement process*, unpublished Ph.D. thesis, University of Wales, 1985.

McGoldrick, A. and Cooper, C., Early retirement:
the appeal and the reality, Personnel Management,
July 1978.

MacKenzie, H., The third statistical account of
Scotland: the City of Aberdeen, Oliver and Boyd,
Edinburgh, 1953.

Mann, F. and Williams, L., Organizational impact of
white collar automation, in Faunce, W. (ed),
Readings in industrial sociology, Appleton-
Century-Crofts, New York, 1967.

Marsden, D. and Duff, E., Workless, Penguin,
Harmondsworth, 1975.

Martin, R. and Fryer, R., Redundancy and paternalistic capitalism: a study in the sociology of
work, George Allen and Unwin, London, 1973.

Mead, M., Coming of age in Samoa, Penguin, Harmondsworth, 1966.

Meadows, W., Local government: discretion with
accountability, in Jackson, P. (ed), Government
policy initiatives 1979-80: some case studies
in public administration, Royal Institute of
Public Administration, London, 1981.

Military Retirement System: Hearing before the
task force on entitlements, uncontrollables and
indexing of the Committee on the Budget, House
of Representatives, Serial no. TF8-6, Government
Printing Office, Washington D.C., 1983.

Miller, H., The ageing countryman: a socio-medical
report of old age in a country practice,
National Corporation for the Care of Old People,
London, 1963.

Minutes of City of Aberdeen District Council 1977-
1980, Part II 1978-1979, Aberdeen District
Council.

Minutes of City of Aberdeen District Council,
unbound, 17 October 1983.

Minutes of City of Aberdeen District Council,
unbound, 2 December 1985.

Mitchell-Gill, A., The families of Moir and Byres,
Wyllie and Son, Aberdeen, 1885.

Modernisation of local government in Scotland (The),
White Paper, Cmnd. 2067, Scottish Office, HMSO,
Edinburgh, 1963.

Moore, S., Old age in a life-term arena, in
Myerhoff, B. and Simic, A. (eds), Life's career -
aging:cultural variations in growing old, Sage,
Beverly Hills, 1978.

Morgan, D., The Denburn - from source to sea:
Part 29, at Poynernook with Piries, Leopard, no.
90, June 1983.

Morgan, P., *The annals of Woodside and Newhills*,
Wyllie and Son, 1886.

Musgrove, F. and Middleton, R., Rites of passage and
the meaning of age in three contrasted social
groups: professional footballers, teachers, and
Methodist ministers, *British Journal of Sociology*,
vol. 32, no. 1, March 1981.

Musto, D. and Benison, S., Studies on the accuracy
of oral interviews, Fourth National Colloquium
on Oral History, U.S. Oral History Association,
mimeo, 1969.

*New Local Authorities: Management and Structure
(The)*, (The Bains Report), HMSO, London, 1972.

*New Scottish Local Authorities: Organisation and
Management Structures (The)*, (The Paterson Report),
HMSO, Edinburgh, 1973.

Norris, G., Industrial paternalist capitalism and
local labour markets, *Sociology*, vol. 12, no. 3,
September 1978.

Paper, UK paper industry crippled by high energy
prices, 4 October 1982.

Paper, UK mills: further declines, 24 January 1983.

Paper Centenary Issue, The British Paper and Board
Industry Federation: a century of service, 1979.

Paper Review of the Year, The industry proves its
resilience, 1975.

Paper Review of the Year, UK stays viable, but ...,
1977.

Paper Review of the Year, It was a poor year for
most and disastrous for some, 1981.

Paper Review of the Year, An unhappy chapter for UK
papermakers, 1982.

Paper Review of the Year, Gloom closes in again,
1983.

Parker, S., *Older workers and retirement*, OPCS/Social
Survey Division, HMSO, London, 1980.

Parker, S., *Work and retirement*, George Allen and
Unwin, London, 1982.

Pearson, M., The transition from work to retirement
(1), *Occupational Psychology*, vol. 31, Part 2,
1957.

Pension Communications Ltd., *Your pension: a guide
to the Local Government Superannuation Scheme*,
Pension Communications Ltd. London, 1979.

Phillipson, C., *The emergence of retirement*,
Working Papers in Sociology, no. 14, University
of Durham, Durham, 1977.

Phillipson, C., *Capitalism and the construction of
old age*, Macmillan, London, 1982.

Pirie, F., <u>Co-operation in production or industrial partnerships</u>, Daily Free Press pamphlet, Aberdeen, September 1884.

Pirie, F., <u>Our commercial competitors in America</u>, Daily Free Press pamphlet, Aberdeen, February 1889.

Pirie and Sons, <u>Catalogue of the Stoneywood Works Library</u>, 1871.

<u>Press and Journal</u> (Aberdeen), Doubled output - fewer machines, 1 December 1967.

<u>Press and Journal</u> (Aberdeen), Prosperous future for N.E. mill, 21 March 1974.

<u>Press and Journal</u> (Aberdeen), Aberdeen District may build own houses, 23 December 1975.

<u>Press and Journal</u> (Aberdeen), City tories suspicious of works' plans, 16 November 1976.

<u>Press and Journal</u> (Aberdeen), Council face painter poser, 8 September 1977.

<u>Press and Journal</u> (Aberdeen), Assurance follows N.E. paper mill jobs loss, 16 January 1981.

<u>Press and Journal</u> (Aberdeen), No entry costs £16,000 a year, 28 July 1983.

Pyke, F., <u>The redundant worker: work, skill and security in an engineering city</u>, Working Papers in Sociology, No. 17, University of Durham, Durham, 1982.

Quinn, J., Job characteristics and early retirement, <u>Industrial Relations</u>, vol. 17, no. 3, October 1978.

<u>Reform of Local Government in Scotland (The)</u>, White Paper, Cmnd. 4583, HMSO, Edinburgh, 1971.

Rhodes, R. and Midwinter, A., <u>Corporate management: the new conventional wisdom in British local government</u>, Studies in Public Policy no. 59, Centre for the Study of Public Policy/ University of Strathclyde, Glasgow, 1980.

Rosen, B. and Jerdee, T., The influence of age stereotypes on managerial decisions, <u>Journal of Applied Psychology</u>, vol. 61, no. 4, 1976.

Roth, J., <u>Timetables</u>, Bobbs-Merrill, Indianapolis, 1963.

Rothwell, R. and Zegveld, W., <u>Technical change and employment</u>, Francis Pinter, London, 1979.

<u>Royal Commission on Local Government in Scotland 1966-1969</u>, (The Wheatley Report), Cmnd. 4150, HMSO, Edinburgh, 1969.

Salaman, G., Some sociological determinants of occupational communities, <u>Sociological Review</u>, vol. 19, no. 1, February 1971 (a).

Salaman, G., Two occupational communities: examples
of a remarkable convergence of work and non-work,
Sociological Review, vol. 19, mo. 3, August 1971
(b).

Secker, J., The construction industry, in Hastings,
S. and Levie, H. (eds), Privatisation ?,
Spokesman, Nottingham, 1983.

Showler, B. and Sinfield, A. (eds), The workless
state, Martin Robertson, Oxford, 1981.

Simic, A.,Winners and losers: ageing Yugoslavs in
a changing world, in Myerhoff, B. and Simic, A.
(eds), op. cit., 1978.

Slater, R., Age discrimination, in Carver, V. and
Liddiard, P. (eds), An ageing population, Hodder
and Stoughton/Open University Press, London, 1978.

SOGAT, Action now!, Society of Graphical and Allied
Trades, Hadleigh, 1981.

Smith, J., Older workers retrained, New Society,
4 July 1974.

Smith, H., Strategies of social research: the
methodological imagination, Prentice Hall,
Englewood Cliffs, N.J., 1975.

Social Trends, no. 16, HMSO, London, 1986.

Taylor, F., The principles of scientific management,
Norton, New York, 1967 edition.

Terborgh, G., Automation hysteria and employment
effects of technological progress, in Marcson,
S. (ed), Automation, alienation and anomie,
Harper and Row, New York, 1970.

Terkel, S., Hard times: an oral history of the
Great Depression, Pantheon/Random House, New
York, 1970.

Thane, K., The muddled history of retiring at 60
and 65, New Society, 3 August 1978.

Thomae, H., Cross-national differences in social
participation: problems of interpretation, in
Havighurst, R. et al, op. cit., 1969.

Thompson, P., Problems of method in oral history,
Oral History, vol. 1, no. 4, 1971.

Tilley, J., Changing prospects for direct labour,
Fabian Tract 445, Fabian Society, London, 1976.

Toshi, K., Recent extensions of retirement age in
Japan, The Gerontologist, vol. 19, no. 5, 1979.

Travers, T., Pay versus jobs: the choice facing
local authorities, Public Money, vol. 2, no. 3,
December 1982.

Travers, T., Local government demanning, Public
Money, vol. 3, no. 1, June 1983.

T.U.C., <u>Draft TUC evidence to House of Commons Social Services Select Committee on retirement age</u>, Trades Union Congress, (unpublished), circa 1981.

Twente, E., <u>Never too old</u>, Jossey-Bass, San Fransisco, 1970.

Vidich, A., Participant observation and the collection and interpretation of data, in McCall, G. and Simmons, J. (eds), <u>Issues in participant observation: a text and reader</u>, Addison-Wesley, Reading (Massachusetts), 1969.

Walker, A., The social consequences of early retirement, <u>The Political Quarterly</u>, vol. 53, no. 1, 1982.

Walsh, K., Manpower in local government, <u>Local Government Studies</u>, vol. 9, no. 4, August 1983.

Ward, R., <u>The aging experience: an introduction to social gerontology</u>, Lippincott, New York, 1979.

Ward, S., Early retirement - what it really means, <u>Labour Research</u>, August 1981

Wedderburn, D., <u>Redundancy and railwaymen</u>, Cambridge University Press, Cambridge, 1965.

Wedderburn, D., Unemployment in the seventies, in Butterworth, E. and Weir, D. (eds), <u>Social problems in modern Britain</u>, Fontana, London, 1976.

Wedderburn, D., Social factors in satisfaction with rotating shifts, in Colquhoun, W. and Rutenfranz, J. (eds), <u>Studies in shiftwork</u>, Taylor and Francis, London, 1980.

White, M. and Trevor, M., <u>Under Japanese management: the experience of British workers</u>, Heinemann, London, 1983.

Whyte, W., Moving up and down in the world, in Glaser, B. (ed), <u>Organizational careers: a source book for theory</u>, Aldine, Chicago, 1968.

Wiggins Teape (UK) plc, <u>Stoneywood Today</u>, (works magazine), Summer 1981.

Wright, J. and Hamilton, R., Work satisfaction and age: some evidence for the 'job change' hypothesis, <u>Social Forces</u>, vol. 56, 1978.

Wood, S., Managerial reactions to job redundancy through early retirements, <u>Sociological Review</u>, vol. 28, no. 4, 1980.